Thirty-three Years
to Conception

A Voice from the Street

2018 Edition

By Daniel S. Pollock, as told to Evelyn N. Pollock

"I know that I am worth more than absolutely nothing."
Daniel Pollock

Co Authors: Daniel S. Pollock, Evelyn N. Pollock

Graphic Designer and Publisher: Beverly Pearl
Editors: Gwynn Scheltema and Ruth E. Walker

The cover photo of Daniel was taken by his mom at Toronto Lakeshore two months after he came off the street. The cover background photo shows the doorway at Church Street and Shuter Street in Toronto where Daniel slept when he was homeless.

Email: pollockconsulting@bellnet.ca

ISBN: 978-1-387-52838-7

H&S Le Temps H&S Times
http://www.tempshstimes.com/

ACKNOWLEDGEMENTS

Special thanks to the following people for their encouragement, support and honest feedback:

Manuscript Readers:
Veronika and Ron Armstrong
Barbara Baker
Karen Brodie
Louise Calvert-Dale
Johnna Dalrymple
Nora Lippa
Susan McTavish
Ken Orenstein
Beverly Pearl
David Pollock
Karen Pollock
Brenda Reid
Gwynn Scheltema
Ruth E. Walker

Mentors:
David Pollock
John Forrest
Prose and Cons Writers' Group

This is a true story; however, most names in this book have been changed to protect the identities of individuals.

In memory of Daniel S. Pollock, April 24, 1974 to September 15, 2017

DEDICATION

To my mother - your love, encouragement and hope have been given to me despite the worrying, sleepless nights, and hell on earth I have given you. Any other person would have lost her mind and gone insane. You have done all of this just so you could have a son who felt loved and cherished. I'm sorry and I do feel cherished. Without your love this book wouldn't have happened. You are my guardian angel. I think you are one of the reasons that I'm still here and I love you.

To my father - you are, without a doubt the definition of a great father. You have shown me unconditional love, proper discipline, and you have provided an environment that every child would want and I love you.

To my sister - what can I say but sorry for the times I wasn't there by your side to protect and love you and be your big brother and friend. I love you and I want you in my life.

I also dedicate this book to my late grandparents, Bubby Libby and Zaidy Jack. They were like a second set of parents to me and I know they loved me unconditionally. I miss you both and you will always be with me.

Daniel S. Pollock

PREFACE

This story is for my parents. I hope it answers their questions about where I was and what I was doing when I disappeared for long periods of time between the ages of fifteen and thirty-three. I know they spent many sleepless nights worrying about me and I owe them answers.

I regret that I have spent so much of my life just totally abusing myself and everybody else around me. I was filled with total greed and anger towards everyone. I was stubborn and always wanted to be right and everything had to be about me.

I always imagined that my parents and I were in two different worlds. I was a drug addict, homeless and on the street. I had no hopes, no dreams, no future and no destiny. Meanwhile, I thought my parents were living an upper class lifestyle and enjoying their lives, as they deserved to. I never thought about, or understood, how much my parents worried about me, how much despair they suffered because of me, or how their lives were forever affected by my actions.

By dictating this story, for the first time in my life I am doing something that has meaning. My parents have a right to know about my life. They need to know that what happened to me was never their fault. I also hope that this story will help others. If it does, then I will know that the last eighteen years of my life were not totally wasted.

Contents

1 THE BEGINNING   1

2 DROPPING OUT   5

3 INDEPENDENCE   9

4 TRYING COCAINE   13

5 NICOLE - A LIFELINE   17

6 REHAB TIMES TWO   21

7 FATHERS AND SONS   25

8 LOSING JACKSON   31

9 AN ADDICT'S DREAM   35

10 MOMENTS OF REFLECTION   39

11 A NEW PERSONA   43

12 IMPORTING DRUGS   49

13 DRUGS OF CHOICE 53

14 OFF TO JAMAICA 59

15 STUCK IN ANTIGUA 63

16 ALL GOOD THINGS END 69

17 WAITING FOR TRIAL 73

18 DOING TIME 77

19 MEETING BRITTANY 83

20 DOWNHILL AGAIN 87

21 NEAR DEATH 91

22 CRY FOR HELP - DETOX 97

23 HITTING BOTTOM 101

24 REHAB IN QUEBEC 105

25 HOMELESS 111

26 LIFE ON THE STREET 119

27 PANHANDLER REFLECTIONS 125

28 PANHANDLING TICKETS 129

29 CHANCE TO START OVER 133

30 STREETS TO HOME   137

   AFTERWORD   143

   FINAL FAREWELL   144

Chapter 1

THE BEGINNING

It all began back in April 1974, on the day that my birth mother took her first look at me, held me in her arms and then passed me on to my real mother. Ever since then my real mother has held me, cherished me and showered me with all the love that she could.

I was adopted when I was five days old by a family that had lots of love to give. My father was a doctor and my mother was a teacher, so their financial situation was never anything to worry about. They probably really wanted me and loved me - I am sure they did.

Looking through pictures from my youth, I see that my parents gave me anything and everything that a child could ever want, and then some. I see their smiles and see me in their arms. My grandparents were also a big part of my life, and they are in many of the photos.

My father's parents passed away early in my life. My mother's parents, Libby and Jack, were like second parents to me. As I grew up, I realized this more and more. I cherished the sanctuary they had for me. Their door was always open, no matter what happened. No matter what I did, no matter what time it was, I always had a place to go and I always had something to eat. My grandmother, Bubby Libby, was special. She had a way of knowing when I had done something wrong and gave me that look - no yelling, arguing or punishments. Usually, I ended up with a big hug, a kiss and something to eat.

I don't know why, but when I was younger, I always felt awkward and out of place; not with my parents, grandparents or sister, but with some of my cousins and other relatives. I usually felt the same thing in school. I'm not sure what it was and I still can't pinpoint why I always felt not liked and just not with the in crowd, so to speak, from Grade One all the way up.

We were well-to-do with an above-average lifestyle. I'd watch TV and see families with less, struggle to become something so they could get out of their poor neighbourhoods. In TV families, I saw bonds of love, joy and glee when they finally made it through their hardships.

In my family, there just wasn't any sort of struggle to get out of a neighbourhood or to gain something. For some reason, that didn't really feel like family to me. A family, I thought, should be close and tight. I always got the impression that my parents were more worried about appearances and what other people would think than they were about dealing with the issues at hand. When people came over to our house, it always seemed that any problem that I was having was brushed aside or never mentioned. To everybody else everything was fine. I always thought that was kind of bullshit; we should have been dealing with the issues and not trying to be fake.

From a very young age, I always rebelled and argued with my parents and could never understand why. I had everything that anybody could want - loving parents, a loving younger sister and grandparents who adored me. For some reason, I always seemed to have the attitude that I was in charge - it was my way or no way.

In school, I tried to be the class clown and make people laugh. I also tried to be the tough guy, the bully and semi-rebellious. I was always anti-authority at home, at school and, later on, with the police. I don't know why. It just seemed like it was something in my nature.

Time moved on. I started Grade Seven at Arlington Senior Public School with kids from a more diverse community. The school was just across the park from our house. Before this, in elementary school, I had always been with kids from the same neighbourhood, the same religion, and the same financial background, so I never really saw any diversity.

In Grade Seven and Eight, I started meeting people from different ethnic backgrounds, different faiths and different rungs of the financial ladder. I met bad kids who were tough, gangsters, wannabe gangsters, nice kids, geeky kids, and all those different types that are in junior high and high school.

I was always pulled towards people from lower income families who seemed to have to struggle to get ahead. I hung around with them, on the other side of tracks, so to speak, being rebellious, causing trouble, running around, smoking cigarettes and doing all sorts of stuff that the kids in my area weren't doing. I just kind of felt that the people from my local neighbourhood were not as interesting, not as exciting, not doing anything, and that led me to even more anti-authority behaviour.

I wasn't pressured into doing anything when I was a child.

I was never sexually or physically abused. None of my friends, at any point, ever forced me into doing anything that I really didn't want to do. In fact, when I finally found the clique where I fit in, I was more of a leader than a follower. I started skipping classes, getting detentions, getting suspended and pushing the envelope everywhere I went and not thinking much about it.

I don't know if that stemmed from coming from a family that could afford to travel to different places on weekends and on vacations, and not really having to worry about things. I just figured, maybe from movies, that the rich are always rich, that nothing ever goes wrong. It doesn't matter what they do, or when they do it. They always end up with the car, the family and the house.

Maybe I felt that way because, no matter how much trouble I got into, the worst thing that ever happened to me was that a toy was taken away, or I wasn't allowed to watch TV. At the end of the week we still went away to the country and I was still able to play hockey, which was my greatest passion.

Chapter 2

DROPPING OUT

In the Jewish faith, you have a Bar Mitzvah when you are thirteen and that is considered to be the age that you become a man. I turned thirteen towards the end of Grade Seven. It was around that time that I began to meet lots of people from different areas of the city, different financial backgrounds, different ethnic groups and different religions. I just thought that I was getting cultured and starting to live life.

By the end of Grade Eight, at the age of fourteen, I was smoking pot, dropping acid, going to parks, tripping out, going to parties and having good, wholesome fun. It was not necessarily legal, but it was what kids did. There wasn't so much drinking as there was marijuana, hash, acid, mushrooms and stuff like that.

At first, I hung around in the Eglinton and Bathurst area. Then I started hanging out down towards Dufferin Street with another crowd, smoking pot, having fun. It was just the harmless sort of fun that kids have; not the big consequential things like stealing, robbing or vandalizing.

I just figured that was what life was about and I was going to have as much fun as I could for as long as possible. I didn't realize that while I was having fun with different people on different days, everybody else was still going to school and getting ahead. Unlike me, they were in control of themselves.

After my parents figured out that I wasn't getting along in the regular public school system, they sent me to a private high school for Grade Nine, down in the east end of the city by Eglinton and Victoria Park.

Metro Prep Academy was supposed to be a high school for kids that didn't get along well in the public school system. There were smaller classes and there was more individual attention from the teachers. But all that happened there was that I was with other kids from all over the city who were also skipping school. Basically, classes were small because everyone who was supposed to be there was skipping classes and smoking pot behind the school.

Sometimes, I would stay out all weekend. Of course, I was having problems with my family because I was pushing the limits. When I finally came home, there would be confrontations and I would argue, yell and scream.

My mom tried showing affection and love, thinking that would stop me from what I was doing. Unfortunately, I was just a rebellious kid. Nothing was going to stop me from doing what I wanted. No matter what it took, I was prepared to suffer any consequence thrown at me in order to do what I wanted, when I wanted.

In Grade Nine, I started hanging around with gangs downtown. In those days, there were the Untouchables and bigger crowds. There were bad kids, from all over the city, skipping school, hanging out together and causing trouble.

Personally, I never enjoyed school and always liked to skip classes. It's weird because I hung around with the kids skipping school, but I was the only one basically skipping school every day.

I was going all the way from my house at Bathurst and Eglinton to the school at Eglinton and Victoria Park just to smoke pot and skip school. I figured it really didn't make sense. So I dropped out of Grade Nine just before the exams at end the of the school year. By that time, I was over fifteen and there was nothing my parents could do about it.

Now that I look back, I realize that there were different kids, at different times, skipping some school. They weren't doing it all the time like I was.

Later on, I realized that most of those kids didn't drop out of school like I did. They went on to finish high school, go to college and get ahead in life.

Maybe I acted that way because I had an addictive personality that drew me to be bad, to take drugs and to be in an altered state - all the stuff that determined who I was then and who I am today, and continues to lead me to do the things that I do.

Maybe that, right there, was the turning point of my life.

Chapter 3

INDEPENDENCE

As a kid I loved to play hockey, to ski and to skateboard, and I was good at sports. My family always went skiing together on weekends, but I argued with my parents because I just wanted to stay home and hang out with my friends.

At the age of fifteen, I found a part-time job at a ski and skateboard shop a few blocks from our house. There, I got to know different people and I sort of fit into that group. There was more pot smoking. Drinking was introduced a bit more. By that time, I had dropped out of school.

I couldn't legally work full-time until the age of sixteen. My parents kept hoping that I would go back to school. When I was offered a full-time job at the skateboard shop, my mom made me apply to the board of education to get an Early School Leaving Permit, so I could legally work and, at least from my mother's point of view, still get monitored by a teacher from the board of education.

Before I was fifteen-and-a-half, I was working full-time and making money. I decided to move out to live with one of the older guys who worked at the skateboard shop. He lived with a couple of other people in a rented house at Victoria Park and Danforth, on a street called St. Dunstan.

Basically, it was a skateboard party-house, meaning that four of us lived there and all we did was party, smoke pot and drink. We would wake up, get dressed for work, smoke a big joint, and drink a couple of cups of coffee. We'd get to work at 7:30 or 8:00 o'clock in the morning. Everybody at work smoked pot. So we smoked joints throughout the day and then we'd take the bus home.

With three other roommates and all their friends, I'd come home to twenty or thirty people in the house. Everybody was stoned already, skateboarding on the street out front, causing trouble in the neighbourhood, and passing out. Basically, that was all my life was - sitting around, getting wasted, having fun.

Some of these people were a lot older than me and a little more settled in their lives and finances because they had worked for a longer period of time. I was a young kid, thinking that everything was great because I was making five or six dollars an hour. And, I was accepted by these older people as I got drunk, stoned on acid, and puked.

Now that I look back, I realize how young I was then. Sometimes it was fun and sometimes it wasn't. What I basically did was throw away my life slowly, slowly, slowly, while thinking that, in my cozy life, nothing could ever go wrong and I'd always be at that level. I didn't realize that I was slowly being brought down to absolutely nothing. It was a shame.

I had my own room in a house. I'd have girls over and they'd spend the night. We partied at home and then we went to work, which was more like partying than work. I got paid and to my 15-year-old mentality, I was living the great life. I thought it was never going to end.

Sooner or later what happened? I lost my job at the skateboard shop. All of a sudden it was crunch time. So what did I do? Instead of paying my rent with my separation pay, I bought more dope, more pot, and more beer, like nothing had changed, like nothing was wrong, like I'd been doing my whole life.

As usual, I avoided confrontations and problems, even problems happening to me. In fact, I chose to deny that problems even existed. Next thing I knew, my roommates were asking me for my rent. I didn't have the money but didn't say so. I said that I had found someone else to move in. Then I had to go find this someone else. Thank God, for some reason, things just seemed to fall into place for me. I found someone. So what happened? The guy moved in and said he was going to give me last month's rent. But he didn't. Instead, he hit the highway without paying and he took some of our stuff.

There I was, just a few months after leaving home, and I had to move back. By then I was over sixteen. Once again I was back to arguing with my parents because, hey, I'm a man now. I've lived on my own. I've paid my own bills. I had my own place. I did what I wanted. Now I was back in my parents' house, fighting with them, being stubborn, and wanting to do whatever I wanted. I couldn't handle it. In my mind, I didn't have to be there anymore. I didn't want to be there anymore.

My parents didn't know what to do. They were worrying, crying and upset. I was probably just destroying them - and that was only the beginning. I made things so bad for everyone that they decided, okay, if Daniel wants to be by himself, so Daniel will be by himself.

They helped me rent a room in a rooming house on Albany

Avenue, down at Bathurst and Bloor. I started making friends again with some of the people that I had hung around with at Bathurst and Eglinton, decent people. Once again I had a room. It was a small room, but it was a place for people to come to smoke their pot, have a good time, and party. It was Dan's party house once again.

People came, not because I was me, but because I had a place where anybody could come inside and do what they wanted. To me that felt great.

There, I met Liza who was also a problem kid, had lost her place and had no place to go. I was almost sixteen. She was a couple of years older than me. I invited her to come and stay with me. She was a girl. I was going to get lucky - yadda, yadda - next thing I knew she showed up with her boyfriend. That was okay. I was a nice guy and not too forward. I'd never been a pushy person. I'd always waited for girls to approach me and then I'd talk to them.

I would party and drink with Liza and her boyfriend until they went out. Then my other friends would come over and smoke pot. My two groups of friends didn't get along. Some of these new people didn't even really like me too much. I never understood why, because I'm very good at adapting to different people. No matter where I am, I've always been able to blend in. Then again that could be from when I was younger and my parents taught me how to be very polite, to have good manners and to deal with people of different backgrounds.

Chapter 4

TRYING COCAINE

All of a sudden I was introduced to cocaine. It wasn't pushed on me. No one ever tempted me to try it. Nobody ever dared me to try it. There was no peer pressure. It was just something that I thought I wanted to do, and that was that. Actually, I pretended that I had done it before.

Any time I did something like drugs, or drinking, or anything that I had never done before, I never, ever, let anybody know that it was my first time. Why? I don't know. Maybe I was afraid someone would try to do the right thing by stopping me and I just didn't want to be denied.

I started doing a few lines of cocaine here and there. When people from my home neighbourhood came over to smoke pot, I'd hide the fact that I'd done cocaine. They never knew.

Usually you hide things from your parents. The next thing I knew, I was hiding things from my friends.

Slowly but surely I started to do more cocaine. I started to weed out the people who, a couple of years back, I had wanted to accept me and be my friends. Why? Because when it came to them, I was embarrassed about what I was doing. I hated drama and I hated being wrong and I hated people feeling sorry for me. So, to keep doing things I shouldn't have been doing, I started to weed out the people who would make me think realistically and try to get me to do something better with my life.

Next thing you know, the rent was due and I wasn't trying to get on welfare like I was supposed to. Of course, I didn't tell the people who were staying with me. I didn't tell my parents. I didn't tell anybody.

Everything was going well, just like it should, until the landlord asked when I was going to pay the rent. I put off the landlord and put off the landlord. He threatened eviction and I still didn't say anything to anybody. I acted like nothing had happened and everything was great. Why? Because I was afraid that the party might come to an end; I had always made it through before, so I guess I figured, why couldn't I do it again?

It got to the point where Liza and her boyfriend, the people who had been living on my floor, found their own place and moved out. The next thing I knew, the landlord came over and shut off the power. I turned the power back on. It was sort of a war.

Then finally, a construction guy knocked on my door and told me that I had to get out. I looked at him and he didn't look like the landlord, or like a relative of the landlord. He was a white guy and the landlord was an East Indian.

I'm like, "No!"

He's like, "Yeah, you have five minutes to get out. This building has been sold, there are new owners and we're here to tear down the house and rebuild it."

I almost freaked. I didn't know what to do. I wasn't talking to my parents. I had lost all my decent friends and I was starting to get wired with cocaine.

The people who had been living with me were worldlier than me - meaning that they were older and had been on their own for a little bit longer and knew what to do in certain situations - they had taken off.

What was I to do?

I looked outside and saw the bulldozer and the construction crew waiting for me to grab whatever I could and leave. The rest was going to become garbage. I walked.

Thank God I was only at Bathurst and Bloor and Liza and her boyfriend - the people who had been living with me - were at Spadina and Dupont. I walked over there carrying everything I had. I broke down and cried. Then I swore - the tough guy going soft.

The next thing I knew, I had moved in with them. Things were okay because, hey, I had let them stay with me, so they might as well let me stay with them.

I figured that as long as I didn't stay any longer than they had stayed with me, there wouldn't be any friction. That was my mentality. I figured that if I could find ways to get money and participate in payments for the partying, then why not? When one person doesn't have any money and the other person does, it just helps the party to keep going on longer, right?

By that point, I was getting in deeper and deeper. As a kid, I was afraid of needles - didn't want them, didn't let anyone near me with a needle.

Now that I was a tough guy on my own with no cares in the world, I thought, "Why not try coke? Everyone else is doing it."

The first time I tried injecting coke, I asked someone else to give me my first hit. I guess you'd call it a smash. I fell in love with the rush.

Next thing I knew, all I was doing was drinking and smashing coke. It got to the point where my arms were so sore because I kept smashing in the same spots and got scabs. I smashed the scabs and it was just a horrible sight.

Chapter 5

NICOLE - A LIFELINE

Another twist to my life came along. Even though it wasn't permanent, it might have been a message - sort of a lifeline thrown out to me. I met a girl named Nicole who had been kicked out of her house. I was seventeen-and-a-half. She was a year older.

Nicole came from a pretty decent family. She kind of fancied me and I thought she was kind of cute. Most of the time, Liza and her boyfriend and Nicole and I all hung out together. They were a little bit older than us and into the cocaine and other stuff. When Nicole met me, I was doing cocaine. She liked me, but I wasn't going to stop doing cocaine for her. At the same time, I wanted to impress her. Nicole broke up with her boyfriend and we started dating.

Nicole was a very heavy drinker. She had never done coke and she rarely smoked pot or hash or did acid. She was an alcoholic and I liked to drink. So we drank together and had fun. We partied and partied and partied until the two of us moved out of that place and in with another guy and his son

17

down in Kensington Market.

The reason I say that Nicole was a lifeline from God, is that she didn't do drugs. But this guy we moved in with smoked crack, so I started smoking crack.

I slowed down on smashing dope, except when I visited our old housemates, or when I was by myself and had extra money. The rest of my welfare money I spent on booze for me and Nicole, and on a little bit of crack on the side for me and this guy.

Actually, I felt really, really bad when I let Nicole use crack. Finally, I had someone who wanted to be with me, who was not using drugs and I had the opportunity to break free and just try to be happy with this person, even if it wasn't meant to be a long-term thing. Instead, I was the one who let her get started on crack. At the time, she was my way out of that little circle of crack and I didn't see it.

The drugs - the rock and the crack - started getting more of a grip on me. It got the point where I became greedy with Nicole. I had never been greedy before, but I became so greedy that I stopped sharing my crack with her. I hid it when I had it.

I made sure that I split the booze 50/50. If I had six beers, Nicole got three; twelve beers, she got six. I shared everything else but my cocaine. Eventually, I stopped sharing with her all together. Although that was my downfall, it was a blessing because it prevented her from getting addicted to crack.

She already had an alcohol problem. In a roundabout way, thank God I became greedy. No one else deserved to go down the road that I was following.

We moved back to the Coxwell area in the east end of the city. My cocaine habit grew and grew and grew. At the time,

Nicole was still working as a cashier in a store. She never knew about my cocaine. When I got it, I didn't tell her. I spent all my money on cocaine. Her money was spent on booze. So I still got my booze and was able to do more and more and more cocaine on my own.

Periodically, I called my parents from a payphone and we fought and argued. It seemed that I only called my parents to ask for something. I figured they didn't want to hear from me all the time. I'm sure they knew what I was up to. Not knowing where I was, or if I was alive, was probably destroying them. Sometimes, I phoned them just so they got to hear where I was at. But, worrying hits twice as hard when you finally hear a person's voice and then he's gone again. It seemed that every time I talked to them, it was to get food or money.

I kept making promises to get help, just so I could get some money for me and Nicole. I didn't realize that my game was growing stale because my addictions masked reality.

At the time, I didn't think my parents knew what was going on. I was stupid enough to believe that nobody knew anything - nobody knew I was drinking and nobody knew I was getting high.

Now that I look back, how stupid could I have been? I was a pretty intelligent guy. How could I have been so stupid to think that nobody knew what was going on?

Anyway, Nicole and I moved again, to Dupont and Symington in the west end of the city. We got ourselves a little basement apartment - just the two of us. Finally we got to spend time alone in our home. Everything was ours.

She was working and I wasn't, so during the day I found ways to feed my cocaine habit by myself. At night she came home with extra money that she had taken from the till at her job. Sometimes she bought booze. My alcohol problem grew with hers.

We got to the point where every day we drank a forty-ounce bottle of alcohol - the raw alcohol you use for punch. When we finished that at about 10 o'clock at night, we would hit the neighbourhood bar at Symington and Dupont where beer was $1.75 and a shot was $2.00. Believe it or not, we stayed there until closing every night of the week. You can imagine how fast my alcohol addiction was progressing.

Anyway, Nicole eventually lost her job and was at home all day. As a couple, we had applied for and were receiving welfare, but when two people have an alcohol habit like we did, never mind the drug habit, welfare just didn't cut it.

We had a dog and didn't know how to look after it. There were times we panhandled on the street with the dog just to make ends meet. I tried to manipulate my parents for help again, but they had kind of caught on by then. They told me they would only help me if I signed myself into an addiction rehabilitation program.

By then, I was eighteen and Nicole was nineteen.

A few days later, playing on my parents' hopes and dreams for me, I called them back and told them I was sick of everything I was doing and I needed help.

I told them I wanted to go into rehab, but I didn't want my girlfriend, Nicole, to end up on the street.

I told them that I wanted to make sure that our rent was paid, so we could keep our place and not get evicted.

I told them that I was going to change my life.

Chapter 6

REHAB TIMES TWO

As I said, I'm good at talking. Sure enough, my parents said that as long as I went to rehab, they would pay our rent at the end of that month. Boom! I was in like Flynn. Not only was I going on a vacation to rehab for a month, where I would have a nice warm place to stay, with food, but our rent would be paid!

I thought to myself, "You never know, it might help."

But I didn't know what rehab was for. I didn't want to stop drinking. I just wanted money for rent and food.

My mom drove me to the Addiction Research Foundation where I signed myself into a 28-day in-patient program. I kept in touch with my parents by phone and they dropped off some clean clothes and cigarettes to help me out. Nicole got to visit a couple of times and we talked on the phone every day.

As soon as I got out, my parents kept their promise and paid the rent money to the landlord. It was a bad day. First thing I did was go to the beer store. It only took me a couple of days to get back into coke.

Since I had been clean for a month, my greed wasn't there, so I shared a little bit with Nicole. It didn't take long for the crack to grab hold of me again and my sharing with Nicole wasn't doing her a favour.

Things were not really okay. We fought periodically about her being in the apartment by herself for the month I was in rehab. I worried about her ex-boyfriend who used to abuse her and was now in touch again. I thought about the things she did with me while still with him, and wondered if she would do those things with him while with me.

After I got out of rehab, he popped his head around our apartment every now and then. We'd have cans of booze on the weekends and he'd show up. Nicole talked to him and made him comfortable. The situation had a very bad vibe. After a few months everything went to hell. We stopped eating. We drank and tried to get dope. We ripped people off, pissed people off and started fights on the street. I became a miserable, miserable person.

Then I decided, "Hey, you know what? Now that I knew how to get into this Addiction Research Foundation program, why not try it one more time - maybe for real?"

After being in rehab again for a couple of weeks, I called my house. Nicole told me that she had gone to the clinic and found out that she was pregnant.

Now there's an excuse for me to leave rehab, right?

I asked for an emergency pass. The staff refused, so I stayed in rehab.

Then I called my parents and told them that Nicole was pregnant.

They stepped up to the plate from the get-go. Mom was worried but, I guess she was also kind of happy about having a grandchild and happy that I was still in rehab.

This time I finished the program. I was excited and I was ready to make some changes in my life.

Chapter 7

FATHERS AND SONS

My dad was appalled when he learned that Nicole was pregnant. The first thing he thought about was an abortion. I learned many months later that, from day one, my dad suspected that the baby wasn't mine. It would have been nice if he had told me that at the time.

I always got along with my father better than my mother. Maybe it was because he was quiet and didn't get really involved. Sometimes, it almost seemed like he was on my side when I argued with my mother. Now I realize that he was telling Mom to just leave me alone. At the time I thought, "Okay, he agrees with me and I'm right." But now I understand that he just wanted the arguments to end and not hear my bullshit. I said the same old things over and over again and I did nothing but hurt my family.

Things got better between Nicole and me. She was pregnant with my baby and I did everything I could to help. I went to prenatal classes with her. We practised the breathing exercises together and, thanks to my dad, I got a good job as a maintenance worker in a downtown hotel.

Nicole started slowing down on her drinking, which I encouraged, and I started drinking only beer. No longer did we drink forty ounces of liquor and then go out for beer. We just had beer at home, bought things for the baby and tried to get along. I spent every cent that I made on rent, food and clothes for her and our baby.

We moved north to a bigger apartment on a street called Bogart, up in the Bathurst and Sheppard area. It was a pretty decent one-bedroom apartment. My parents helped us out with second-hand furniture. I worked throughout the pregnancy and paid the rent on time.

Our baby was born in early October and we named him Jackson, after my grandfather. That child became my life. After he was born I changed almost 180 degrees for the better. I mean I lived for him.

A few months after Jackson was born, after a year of working, I lost my job again. So what did Nicole and I do? We went back on welfare. As a couple with one child we got a little more money. Things started getting rocky again. We began arguing all the time. Nicole's friends said things that made me wonder if Jackson was mine. If he wasn't mine, I wanted him to be mine - I started pressuring her to tell me that he was mine. I felt stress beyond stress.

After one particularly big blow up, Nicole left and took Jackson to her parent's house. Jackson was about eleven months old. After that, she brought him to me three days a week and I gave her $300 at the end of every month.

One day, when she dropped Jackson off, she asked for the money early and I said, "No." I told her she couldn't have it until the next time she picked Jackson up. I told her that the money was for our child and not for her. Much later, I found out that she had wanted the money to go out with her ex-boyfriend - the same guy she had left for me and the same guy who used to beat her up.

When Nicole returned to pick up Jackson she said that the next time I would see him would be in court for a custody battle. I went from having Jackson a couple of days a week to never. Next thing I knew, Nicole was telling the court that I had threatened to take Jackson out of the country. As a result, the court allowed me to see my son for only three hours every two weeks, supervised by one of my parents. It was horrible. Nicole's parents put a restraining order on me to keep me away from their house.

It was a downhill slide for me after that court ruling. I had no job. I stopped paying rent and ignored the eviction letters. One thing led to the next and I was evicted from our apartment on Bogart and had to leave everything behind. I moved back to the Eglinton and Marlee area, into a small basement apartment in a house. Then I got back into the crack and booze really heavy.

I was preparing to see my son for the first time in a few months after all this court shit. The night before I was scheduled to see him, I went to my parents' place and had a huge fight with my mom. I was really high and I lost my temper in a big way.

My mother said, "Okay, I'll pick up Jackson from Nicole tomorrow morning and meet you in front of your place, but you have to call me first so I know you're not high." I didn't have a phone at the time. Well, I sat in front of my place and waited and waited and waited and waited and my mother never showed up.

I thought, great, that bitch Nicole didn't show up to meet my mom. I called my parents' place and listened to the phone ring and ring and ring and ring. There was no answer - same with my mom's cell phone. I didn't know what was going on. I got really pissed off.

I ended up going to my sanctuary - my grandparents' house. Whenever I felt down, no matter what was wrong, I could go there and always feel better. That house was a bubble of love. It didn't matter who you were, the first time you went there, you left feeling like you'd known them forever.

I sat down on their couch and my grandmother asked me if I wanted something to eat. Then she said how beautiful Jackson was. My heart stopped.

"What are you talking about?" It turned out that my mother had picked up the baby and brought him to my grandmother's house. I freaked out and called my mother. She said that I had never called her and I hadn't been where I was supposed to be.

She knew where I was living, whether or not I called her. My house wasn't even a five-minute car drive from my grandparents' place, but she hadn't checked to see if I was home.

Enraged, the next thing I knew, I was at my mom's apartment ready to kill. The security guard saw me outside and called my father. He came downstairs where I was arguing with the security guard.

Then I saw my mom turn her car into the driveway. She was about to pull into the underground garage. She hesitated when she saw me and stopped the car on the ramp. The next thing I knew I was beside her car and I slammed my hand right through her car window.

It was like everything happened in slow motion. I kind

of froze. I hadn't meant to do that but I was so angry. I couldn't believe that the woman who cried on the phone, who supposedly cared about me so much, who worried so much about me, could do something like this. I couldn't believe that my mother would keep my baby from me, especially for my first visit since court. This was the ultimate sin. This baby was keeping me alive, making me want to live for the very first time.

Not long after that, Nicole and I went back to court. She asked for child support and full custody of Jackson. I felt sick about the possibility of losing my son. I told the court that I wanted to know that the baby was really mine. The judge ordered a DNA test.

Six weeks later, the laboratory called my father's office with the DNA results. Jackson wasn't mine.

My heart almost stopped and I froze in time. I'd never felt such an intense loss before. I didn't want to live anymore. No one should ever feel like I felt.

My life went into a total downward spiral.

I imagine that this must be similar to how my parents have felt for many years, because of me. I'm thirty-three years old today, and when I left home at fifteen, they basically lost their son.

Even though they were always there for me, I can only imagine how much pain I gave my parents and grandparents.

Now, looking back, I realize that I must have almost destroyed my parents and my sister. Yet they showed me love every day and carried on with their daily lives despite my behaviour.

Chapter 8

LOSING JACKSON

I still remember the day that I found out that my son wasn't mine. I was with Liza, the friend who had stayed on my floor when I had that room at Bathurst and Bloor.

When my parents got the call from the medical laboratory, they hunted me down at Liza's father's apartment, where we were having some drinks.

I still remember that call. It was the day before I was supposed to have Jackson for one of my supervised visits. On the phone, Mom said that my father was looking for me because they had just got a call from the lab. The DNA test results had come back.

Jackson wasn't mine. Jackson was only sixteen months old.

I remember feeling numb, the news not really sinking in at first. I hung up the phone and told Liza and her dad that I had to go. Being a friend, Liza wanted to come with me to make sure that I was okay.

Liza's father gave us some money. We hopped a cab to my place, picked up more booze, and called the crack dealer. We spent the whole night drinking and smoking about a quarter ounce of crack. We got totally obliterated and had no sleep.

The next morning my mother showed up at the front of my house. She told me that she loved me, said that she was really sorry about the news about Jackson, and gave me a long hug. This was the drunkest that she had ever seen me. She had seen me drunk and high many times, but that day I was spaced out beyond belief and that was the first time she was worried about my emotions, not just about the fact that I was drunk or high.

She gave me some food - obviously there was no way that I had any money for food. Everything had been spent on drugs and alcohol. She also gave me some gift certificates for food at the IGA.

Then, my mother said that my visits with Jackson could continue. She would meet Nicole, pick up Jackson, and bring him to me.

I had thought of Jackson as mine for over two years, including the nine months of Nicole's pregnancy. I had actually watched him being born. I had been in the delivery room, saw his head come out and the placenta afterwards. I was there through it all. I named him after my grandfather, and gave him my last name. That child is still walking around with my name.

My mother was surprised that I didn't want any more visits with him. She didn't understand how much it bothered me that the child I had given my life to, the child who was helping me turn my life around, was not really mine.

After Jackson was born, and Nicole and I had been living together for some time, my life had changed. My addictions sort of went onto the back burner. First of all, I made sure that Jackson had everything, then I fed my addiction, then I fed myself with food. So, basically that child had everything he needed, except - now that I look at it - a fully coherent and emotionally present father.

I can honestly say that whenever I was alone with Jackson and had to take care of him, I never even once drank so much as one sip of alcohol, or smoked one piece of rock, or snorted any coke, or did any pills or any sort of thing like that. I mean, my son was my son.

At the time, I had a distorted view. I felt that my mother didn't realize that I even had emotions. I thought that she was mostly worried that her plans to pick up Jackson were spoiled.

My mother had been in contact with Nicole after court and Nicole wanted me to still see Jackson. Nicole had shown Mom pictures of me with Jackson. In those pictures, I was clearly happy and so was he. According to my mother, Nicole said that every time Jackson saw a photograph of me with him he pointed to it and said, "Daddy, Daddy, Daddy."

That kind of hit me in the gut. In that time period, I was spending all my time drinking and doing drugs with Liza. We were doing crack, so we weren't sleeping. We went to a concert at Ontario Place and Liza bought me a beer. I took one sip and couldn't drink any more. I don't remember the concert - I only remember sweating and hearing loud noise around me. I don't remember even one song that they played. Next thing I knew, the concert was over.

That led to me to sell everything I owned to go on one long bender, consuming as many drugs and as much alcohol as possible.

Some people think that addicts do drugs to forget about things. And you know when addicts are high, they don't think and they don't remember. Drugs just sort of block everything else out. But, for me, no matter how much I drank, no matter how many drugs I did, no matter how high I got from whatever I was on, if something was bothering me emotionally, I continued to think about it. I mean, I stayed upset. At this particular time I knew that drugs were destroying me and I really had no friends - I just had my drugs.

Chapter 9

AN ADDICT'S DREAM

In my mind, I was still having fun. The partying was still a blast. I didn't hate it and I wasn't sick of it. It made me feel young and I was still laughing. Then things took a turn for the worse. People who were users and abusers started coming around. I hung around with worse people and violence slowly but surely crept into my life.

The strong survive and the weak get stepped on, used and abused. I don't know whether or not the people I hung out with thought I was one of those weak-minded people who they could take advantage of - I know I wasn't.

I've never done anything just because someone wanted me to do it. I did what I wanted to do and it just so happened that what I wanted to do was what everyone else wanted to do. No one had to convince me to try anything. I wanted drugs and I was willing to do anything to get them. No one had to convince me to sell anything because I was already figuring it out for myself.

For a little while I continued to live in the same basement

apartment near Eglinton and Marlee. Then I ran into a person I called my lucky friend and my drug friend. He came over every night to smoke his drugs. Seven days a week, pretty much, he came to my house with lots of drugs to smoke for free. He was a nice guy and never used me or took anything from me. He just wanted a place to smoke his drugs and I had a place.

I was willing to smoke his drugs with him. He was a bonus because he came over in the evening, after I had already bought and smoked my own dope by myself during the day. So I was getting high as often as I could on my own and high every night with him.

I worked periodically, earning $50.00 a day. I'd buy six beers, get home at 3 o'clock, drink three of the beers and pass out. My drug dealer would knock on my door to wake me up so I could get high. Then my friend came over.

At that point things were still pretty stable. I was consuming more and more drugs; it was a drug addict's dream. My friend Liza's birthday was in March and her father usually took her on a week-long trip somewhere. He was pretty well off and let her pick where they went. That year she wanted to go to the Dominican Republic, but her father was sick and couldn't go. A nice guy, he asked me to go with her and paid for my trip so that she didn't have to travel alone.

Now, mind you, he didn't know me that well. We had a rapport because I had been friends with his daughter for so long. When he needed help at his house, I cleaned, ran errands for him, bought him his alcohol and did other stuff. He paid me for doing these things and I used the money to buy crack.

Liza's father was a big drinker himself, so every time I went over there, he always ordered me a six-pack or twelve-pack of beer. From him I got my alcohol and left with at least $20 or $40 for crack. I guess he liked me because I was still a well-mannered kid. I have always prided myself on being polite, regardless of the situation. I respect older people as much as they respect me.

So, thanks to her father, Liza and I ended up going on a week-long, completely paid-for vacation to an all-inclusive resort in the Dominican Republic.

Bonus! Back in Toronto, I was a young guy with no job, living in a single room where I faced so much drama, loved to drink and do as many drugs as possible. In the Dominican, I was at a resort with as much free booze as I wanted. I was in Heaven! I had nothing but a good time partying, drinking booze and lying on the beach. What more could I have wanted?

Back home, I was as poor as some of the people living in the Dominican, a third world country. Some of them were poor but had more than I did back home. It was kind of weird and neat.

I had to put on this facade for the other vacationers, from England and all over the world, that I wasn't some poor guy. They had jobs and worked to earn their trip. When they asked what I did in Canada, I couldn't exactly say, "I live on welfare, smoke crack, and drink booze all day." I had to say that I worked, basically lying a little, in order to fit in. But there it goes; I'm easy and good intellectually, so I can adapt to different situations and people around me.

Anyway, Liza was having too much fun, met some local guy and decided to stay there. I came back to Toronto.

Liza ended up staying in the Dominican for a few years, living off her father. Her mother had died when she was very young and the only way her father knew how to take care of her was to give her money and booze.

I thought she had it made. That's kind of what I wanted. I wanted my parents to give me a $60 a day allowance, like she got, plus her 26'er of booze and her rent paid. I figured, "Why can't my parents do this for me?"

Thank God they didn't. Now that I have a clear mind, I understand and I'm glad they didn't enable me by paying for everything and allowing me to do whatever I wanted. That showed that they actually loved me very much.

Chapter 10

MOMENTS OF REFLECTION

Back in Toronto I still had to cope with losing Jackson. Although he was born in 1993, even today I think about him all the time and losing him still hurts.

Sitting here, I think about how I used and abused my parents, the hell that I put them through with my lies and deceits, and how I just stamped out their hopes and dreams for me. I used them just like people I didn't care about and didn't give a shit about.

All I thought about was me - dreaming up cons for money to make my parents think that I was actually living for something and accomplishing something.

I was in my very early twenties and had been away from home for a long time. By the age of twenty-one, I had already dragged my family through hell with my severe addictions to alcohol, crack and injected cocaine. I had lived with a girl who got pregnant, had a son and then lost him, I had gone to the

Dominion Republic with no money, came back, and kept on filling myself with drugs and alcohol.

At the time, I thought my life was fun, although now I'm sure that my parents and other people were going, "You know, this kid is fucked. He's put himself through the ringer."

All of that was child's play compared to what happened next. I started living on the street, begging for money, trying heroin, even injecting heroin.

I finally got caught at the Toronto airport for importing drugs on the way back to Canada from one of my trips down south. As a result, I ended up in jail for months as my case was deferred. In total, I ended up spending almost three years of my life in prison for importing drugs.

Even after all that, I indulged in more alcohol and drug abuse, lost my family totally, didn't communicate with my sister for years, and lost my grandparents who meant so much to me. I saw death, saved somebody's life, and almost got killed in my sleep. Some of this I will tell you later in this story. Other things I can never talk about.

I'm just thankful that I'm still here today. With every sentence and every word that I speak, I think about my parents. Apologies can never be enough for what I've put them through.

Right now, I'm just preparing myself to face the emotional stories that I'm about to share.

While I was living this life, my grandparents were getting older. They moved out of their house and into the same condo building that my parents had moved into three years earlier. Because I loved my grandparents, I continued visiting once, twice or three times a week to help with taking the garbage out, cleaning the humidifier coils, carrying out the recycling and doing odds and ends.

My grandparents were always there for me. No matter what I did, or how bad I was, I could always count on them. They were more than just my grandparents. I loved them as if they were my second set of parents. The love that I saw between them helped me survive.

Through all of this, I still thought that I was having fun and enjoying myself. Nothing seemed to be going wrong and I was happy with what I was doing. I never thought about the future. That's one thing that I was always good at - only thinking about the present. Not even thinking a day ahead can kind of destroy a person.

As I smoked more and more crack and injected more and more cocaine, I stopped paying my rent again.

What did I do? I called my parents with the story that my welfare cheque never came. They pitched in for the rent once again. It only took a month for them to catch on. The next thing I knew, they wanted to hear directly from my welfare worker.

I ended up having to move out, without knowing where to go or what to do. My grandparents welcomed me at their place with open arms. They didn't ask what happened, or why I needed to stay there.

Maybe they had seen how I reacted when my parents questioned me about things, or maybe this was just their kind of loving discipline. Just the look on my grandmother's face told me when I had done something wrong. I think I loved them so much because no matter how upset I felt, I could go there and watch them show the love they had for each other. No matter how bad I felt, just being in their presence made me feel a lot better. Ten minutes after arriving at their house, I forgot all my worries.

After a few days, I moved out because I didn't want to abuse their generosity, like I had done so many times to so many other people.

Chapter 11

A NEW PERSONA

After a while, my friend Liza came back to Canada from the Dominican Republic and was living with her boyfriend in the east end, down by Jones and Dundas. I went and stayed with her for a while. Again my alcohol consumption rose dramatically, as did my cocaine use.

Liza was still living on a daily allowance from her father, who seemed to have quite a few dollars stored away. So, besides the money that I was getting, there was always her money. Other people would come to her house to spend money on drugs and do drugs.

Our food was alcohol and drugs. We rarely ate, and when we did, it was pretty much junk like spaghetti with ketchup. Most of the time, we were high, drunk or sleeping. This carried on for weeks and weeks at a time. We were basically hermits, only going out to the beer store and back, the bank machine and back, the bar and back. Crack had a delivery service so we didn't need to go outside for it.

Liza and her boyfriend fought a lot and I wanted to move

out but, as usual, I wasn't doing anything to make it happen. In other words I just sat around waiting for an opportunity. If one showed up, I would take it and if not, so be it.

Then, I got an offer to make a quick $5,000 Canadian. With my addictions, getting that kind of money all at once was better than I could ever imagine. I might spend that amount over days or weeks, but to actually have a lump sum of $5,000 in my pocket, to spend as I wanted, kind of opened my eyes.

The agreement was to go down to the Islands for a week - Barbados to be exact - to have fun and bring back two kilos of cocaine. My flight and hotel were taken care of, I was given clothes and stuff so that I would look presentable, and I was handed $200 to $300 spending money. I guess it helped that I was well-mannered. All I had to do was bring the drugs back and there would be $5,000 in my pocket.

I went down there. To be honest, I still didn't think about consequences, about coming back, or about getting in trouble with the police. I didn't even think about getting caught in the Islands with that quantity of drugs and what it would do to my family.

Nobody knew where I was. As far as my parents were concerned, I was still somewhere in the city doing whatever. Meanwhile, I was in Barbados sun-tanning, drinking rum, partying, having a good time and about to bring two kilos of cocaine back to Canada.

I flew back, landed in Toronto, and made it through customs fairly easily. My heart raced as I delivered the cocaine. Thinking about the money was almost like a rush in itself. That was the quickest and easiest $5,000 that I had ever made. I was already thinking that maybe I could do it again.

With the money, I went back to Liza's place. I didn't tell

her or her boyfriend what I had done. I just said that I had spent some time with my family. Next thing I knew we were on a three-day drug binge, buying an eight-ball of crack, an eight-ball of powder, a quarter-ounce of crack, and six two-fours of Molson Canadian the moment the beer store opened. Liza's boyfriend wondered where I got the money. I said that it was a gift from my grandparents.

For three days everybody was in a good mood and everybody was having fun, with no bickering. Liza and her boyfriend were in the position that I used to be in - you always acted extra nice to the person with the drugs because the nicer you were, the more drugs you got.

They tried to figure out how I bought so much dope. Anyway, I went out partying with somebody else. We ended up in the Coxwell and Danforth area at a bar where they rented out rooms. A new owner had just taken over and nobody was living above the bar. I went back to Liza's and said that I had rented a room through welfare - I never said that I had any money left.

A few days later, I moved in over the bar. I was the first person to move in after the new owner took over.

I went out to bars and spent as much money as I could. I remember giving the owner of the bar $1,000 cash as a pre-paid bar tab. I felt like the king of the world, a big shooter whose money was never going to run out.

I think it took me three weeks to go through the $5,000 before I was back doing what I did before. That was just enough time for me to have met enough people to know who was and who wasn't an addict. I would get drugs for certain people and let them come to my room to smoke, so by the time my money ran out, I still had that sort of job. By the end of my $5,000, I was able to get credit for my tab in that bar, being the big spender that I was.

At one point my tab went up to $1,300 and I didn't know what to do. Finally, I went down to welfare and got my first and last month's rent. Part went to rent, part to my bar tab, and the rest to partying and doing dope.

Many nights I showed attitude and got into fights in the bar. Tables got thrown over and people got hurt. I got hurt. That started to become part of the fun, part of my new persona. I was fun to be with - a blast. But people who knew me didn't want to get me pissed off because I had quite a temper.

Prior to those days my temper tantrums had mainly consisted of the screaming, yelling, threatening, ranting and raving at my parents. As I got more involved in the drug culture - with the booze, the bars and the rooming houses - I changed.

One day I headed for a park with my friends in the back of a pickup truck. I didn't realize that it had been stolen. As we came out of an alley onto Coxwell, we sideswiped a cabby. He chased us. We finally stopped at Monarch Park, and we got out and the cabby got out. I was all messed up, drunk and high, after taking about ten Valiums. I couldn't really speak, but I grabbed something and swung my arms in the air. The cabby took off. My friend said that he was going to park the truck at a nearby hockey rink.

Next thing I knew, in broad daylight, he was doing donuts in the park. People called the police. Everybody ran away, except for the driver who was trying to re-start the stalled truck. The only person who went back to make sure that his friend got out safely was me. I jumped into the back of the truck and put my hands through the window to try to get the truck started again with a wrench. It didn't happen. I took off. He took off. Next thing I knew, I woke up in the police station.

I ended up in jail. I probably did a week or two of dead time before I got bail from a buddy. Eventually I got a total discharge because the witnesses couldn't place me behind the wheel of the stolen vehicle; I just happened to be in the park at the time. Thank God for my lawyer.

My parents never knew.

Chapter 12

IMPORTING DRUGS

As time went on, the same sort of things kept happening - drunk every day, drugs every day. My everyday routine included walking Danforth, picking fights, getting into fights, hanging out with friends, and just having a good time. I thought of it as harmless fun. My drinking and addictions were bad, but I just thought of myself as hooked.

Then I was offered another job, this time a little bit different and for a little bit more money. I was actually offered $8,000 U.S. to carry the drugs to an Island called St. Vincent, then to Barbados, and then back to Canada.

The first time I went, the people carrying the drugs from Barbados to Toronto bailed. This time, the people bringing them from St. Vincent to Barbados to Canada had bailed. They had actually stashed the drugs on St. Vincent. I got directions to the stash on a little miniature tape. So, I went all the way to Barbados, and then flew over to St. Vincent.

At St. Vincent I stayed in a nice little hotel with a friend, travelled the island as a tourist, and watched a school track and field meet. Basically, I did fun tourist things.

This time was a little more serious, but I didn't think about the consequences - day by day was my philosophy - forget about the future and live in the moment. I was there to party and have a good time.

There I was in St. Vincent, a Canadian who hadn't finished high school, a heavy-duty alcoholic and a cocaine addict, walking through the jungle, or the forest, or whatever they called it, trying to find drugs left behind by someone else two weeks earlier.

Another guy met me there. We could have taken a taxi to the other side of the Island, but we walked. It took us a good forty-five minutes to find the drugs, and I was the one who found the stash. It was up on this little rock face, underneath a bunch of rocks in a little sheltered area. There was a pile of cocaine in half-kilo packages. Holy shit! I'd never seen so many drugs in my entire life. Another envelope, half the size of the others, was the tester.

The people originally supposed to bring it back had taken a tester from each half-kilo to make sure the drugs were real and then they had put the testers into one package that probably weighed a quarter-kilo. On top of the money that I was getting paid, I was told that I could do whatever I wanted with that tester - leave it there, throw it away, or even bring it back to Canada. It was mine, clear and free.

Although I was excited, I kind of regretted finding it. While walking through the forest, I had started to think about the severity of the situation. In a way, I almost hoped that we wouldn't find the drugs because it was much more dangerous to take drugs from one island to another island than it was to just get on a plane and fly back to Canada.

Anyway, I started dipping into the tester, just to try it out. I did line upon line upon line. The next morning, when we were supposed to go back to Barbados, I was sitting in the bathroom high as a kite, without any sleep. The person I was with woke up and yelled at me because my eyes were red. I was just out of it - out of control and unable to eat.

The next thing I knew, the rest of the sample package was flushed down the toilet. I had packages of cocaine strapped to me and we were headed to the little airport in St. Vincent.

We made it to Barbados and got through their customs. At the hotel I slept straight through to the next day. Flushing the rest of the sample down the toilet had been hard for me. I had never imagined that I would willingly and repeatedly send ounces of cocaine down the toilet. We got back to Canada and once again made it through customs as easy as pie.

I had $8,000 U.S. in my pocket and was living the high life once again. I was still living above the same bar and brought back rum for my new friends - actually, they were acquaintances rather than friends. I threw all of my money into my top drawer. I was amazed every time I opened it and saw its bottom covered with twenty-dollar bills.

With the money, I paid off my bar tab and started all over again. I did so much cocaine that I was awake for four and five days straight before I went to sleep. And then I started all over again.

I went to a different bar on Danforth with a friend and a couple of other people. We ordered so much food that the kitchen didn't have enough. I thought that I was a big shooter, a bigwig, sitting there with two tables full of food that we didn't really want to eat. I was just doing it to show off and pretend that I was somebody.

I gained a lot of friends really quickly when I started doing stuff like that. I gained a lot of enemies, too. Then, when the money was gone, only a handful stayed.

Chapter 13

DRUGS OF CHOICE

At the bar, I met a girl who was against the cocaine business, but she loved to drink. This kind of person seemed to be attracted to me - like Nicole had been.

I found it kind of hard to trust women. Usually, when I met a woman, I gave her my all - I put everything into the relationship - went full throttle, opened my heart and expressed my feelings a little too soon, or a little too much. That's my history. After two weeks, a woman basically knows me as well as she should after six months.

Nicole's betrayal had created a little bit of a jealous streak in me. This new girl would disappear for two days without letting me know where she was, then return like nothing happened. There was lots of fighting, yelling, drinking, and doing pills - lots of Librium and Valium. I smoked a lot of crack by going to the washroom or leaving her at the bar and going upstairs and coming back twenty minutes later.

I'd be smoking crack in my room and she'd knock on my door and yell that I was taking too long. I told the people in my room to be very quiet and pretend that we weren't there until she left. That relationship didn't last too long.

I guess I wasn't ready to be in a relationship. I just shouldn't have got so emotionally attached because every time a girl-friend left, I hurt.

I met a lot of decent people back in those days. It was just that the type of drugs that I was doing didn't let me get close to people and people didn't want to get close to me. I was oblivious to reality and thought that everything was hunky dory. My attitude was, "If you want to hang out with me, do so. If you don't want to, so what? I really don't give a shit. Take me for who I am or see you later."

My routine was basically the same every day - wake up towards noon and start drinking and in middle of the afternoon start smoking crack. I did this as long as I possibly could and stopped only when the booze and the drugs ran out, or when I passed out from exhaustion. I had no hope of stopping. Every time I woke up, that was all I wanted to do; I didn't want to go to sleep. It kind of sucked when I wasn't ready for bed but the drugs and alcohol were gone.

I got introduced to more pills - the opiates, including morphine, OxyContin, Dilaudid, and heroin. I started to inject Percocet, Percodan, Tylenol 3s - anything really - for the *downer* sort of high.

My preferences switched, so that opiates - the pills and the heroin - became my addictions and the crack and the coke were more my fun.

It got to the point that I just had to get some opiates into me in order to function and then, hopefully, more to get high - to get buzzed. The coke was just an added pleasure, an added bonus. It's like drinking beer at the bar all the time, then drinking some shots as a treat. That's basically how I figured it. I did as much as I could, as often as I could, to the point where I got sick on heroin every day and couldn't function until I did at least one package, then two packages, and so on and so forth.

The cocaine and heroin crowds are a little bit different. If you have crack on the table a lot of people will either try to steal a little piece of yours, or hide how much they've got. The cocaine crowd seems greedier, potentially more violent, and has a criminal sort of mentality. You smoke a piece of crack and fifteen minutes later you want another one. When it's all gone, you're 'jonesing' so badly, and you want more so badly that, depending on how long you've been doing it, you'd do anything. You'd sell your shoes. You'd steal from your family. You'd rob stores and basically keep going until there was nothing else to steal, you go to jail, or you pass out.

The opium people were more laid-back and relaxed. They understood the sickness that we had. When one opiate addict was sick, another one would do or give something to help.

For instance, I normally did a 100 mg. morphine pill in one smash, one hit. If I got sick and someone else got sick, I'd be more than willing to split my only pill so we could both function, instead of being greedy and running around a corner and doing it all myself.

Doing opiates is such a downer. You get the 'nod' - the itching and the scratching. I couldn't comprehend why some people were violent on opiates, until I really started getting into that addiction. Coke is a speedy thing. Some people would smoke a piece of crack, or do a smash of coke, then clean the house and whatever. When they don't have coke they're lazy and lie around doing nothing.

It was weird, kind of the opposite for me later on in my addiction. When I didn't have my opiates and wasn't feeling too good, or didn't have enough to totally make me not sick, I was lazy. I didn't want to clean. The dishes piled up and things got dirty. Then, the next thing I knew, I was mixing up a *rocket*, which consisted of 200 mg. of morphine, and doing a smash of that, and feeling much better. I'd be up doing the dishes and cleaning the house. If people without that sort of addiction tried doing something like that on even a 100 mg. or 60 mg. pill, they would be sitting on the couch nodding out and scratching their faces off. Yet it helped me get up and be active. It's weird how addictions change.

On opiates you're always searching for the nod and how you can enjoy it. You don't want to do so much that you pass out or nod in and out. Their buzz was my fun, the high that I wanted. The more the nod was, the better. I loved to scratch.

In the drug culture you don't have friends. You have potential enemies. That took me a long time to learn, but when I did, I started to change my life. I hung around with a few people here and there, but you really have no friends, only acquaintances. You're lucky, living on the street, if you actually meet one or two people who you can actually call friends. The rest are just people you're doing dope with.

On the street, if I saw someone getting hurt, I would help them. That's the code of the street. Other than that, the people you do drugs with one day, might be so high the next day, have nothing left, and be *jonesing-out* out and they'll try to rob you of your drugs. That's just life on the street. It happens often. That's what the drug culture is really about.

Anyway, I was still living above the bar and a girl came into my room yelling, "Dan, Dan, so-and-so says they need you."

"What happened?"

"This guy did a smash, fell down and called for you."

He had called for me because I knew what to do when people were overdosing.

I pushed her out of my doorway so hard that she kind of landed on the ground. Then I jumped over her and ran down the hall.

I saw something I'd never seen before in my life. This guy was sitting with his ass on the ground, legs straight out in front of him, his forehead was touching the floor between his legs. Drool was all over the floor. He had urinated and shit in his pants. His lips were blue and he wasn't breathing.

As I gave him mouth-to-mouth, he started coming back. After his breathing was stable, I yelled at him and picked him up in a fireman's carry. I kept talking to him and dragged him around, trying to get him moving, to get his body going. I asked for a lukewarm towel to put on the back of his neck.

I saved this guy's life. Before this, giving anybody CPR had always been a possibility that I dreaded. But when I saw my friend like that, it didn't even faze me that I was covered in his feces. I just wanted to make sure he survived.

When he became coherent and able to walk on his own he was still really, really high. All he could think of was spending the rest of his money on more crack. At that moment I realized what drugs and addictions were about. It's a sickness where twenty minutes after being brought back from death all you want is to smoke another piece of crack.

At the time I was so caught up in the lifestyle that it wasn't a big deal to me that he wanted to smoke crack. But now I can't believe that actually happened. That just blows my mind.

That day, I took a look at myself in the mirror and I realized that I was in bad shape. I was 6-foot-3 inches and 145 pounds, but didn't think that I looked sick. Usually I was over 200 pounds. My arms were sore and always had scabs.

Every time I did a smash, I prepared myself for pain because I kept hitting myself in roughly the same spots. When I first stuck a needle through the scabs I knew that it was going to hurt but that I would soon be high enough and then I wouldn't feel the pain.

It was just sick.

*

Chapter 14

OFF TO JAMAICA

My addiction kept growing and growing and I was offered another vacation.

This time I was off to Jamaica for a little bit of coke. Even though I hadn't ever worked to earn any sort of vacation, I had already visited Dominican Republic, St. Vincent and Barbados, with everything fully paid. I was going south again to have a good time, get loaded and get drunk.

This time, the Jamaican coke was going to be put in the bottom of a suitcase with wheels. I watched the suitcase as it was being professionally made from its bottom to top, including the placement of the foam on top of the cardboard on the bottom. The drugs were wrapped perfectly in carbon paper that confuses x-ray machines; I guess the machines can't pick up the drugs that are in there.

Coming back to Canada from Jamaica I was stopped by airport Customs for an hour and a half. They threw my bag through their x-ray machine nine or ten times, thinking they saw something, then deciding it was nothing.

Five, six, or seven people stared at the x-rays, with most of them saying, "No, no, it's nothing. It's nothing."

They emptied everything out of my bag and started pushing down on it, checking it, questioning me.

I had been through Customs before, so I kept cool. Finally, everyone was sure there was nothing in the suitcase, except one lady. She said she had a feeling that there was something in my bag and wanted to cut it open.

Instead of me panicking and freaking out, I kept my head together. I said, "Before you do anything I want your name, your badge number, your supervisor's number, a phone number where I can make a formal complaint and a promissory note that you're going to pay for my bag, once you destroy it."

Like I said, I'm good at talking.

Anyway, she looked at me in surprise, and then gave me her badge number and all the information pamphlets about where to make complaints, including a phone number. I also convinced them that if they were going to open up my bag, to at least let me to do the cutting. If my bag was going to be destroyed, I wanted to be the one to do it.

So the customs people actually gave me a knife and I made a little incision in the corner at the bottom of the bag.

She said, "Oh, what's the white stuff?"

"Foam lining," I answered. Then, I stupidly asked if she would like me to pick a piece of it out for her.

Of course she said, "Yes".

I don't know how I picked out that piece of foam with a steady hand. Finally, they said I could go.

I actually said to the lady, "I'll tell you what. If my girl-friend is still there waiting for me and I get laid when I get home, because I've been gone for a week, I won't make a complaint. But if she's not there or she's there and I don't get something, I'm making a complaint."

Anyways, when I made my delivery, I took apart the suitcase. If I had cut a millimetre more through the foam, I would have hit the drugs. So that was a good story for me, all fun and games. Thank God.

Again, I hadn't even thought about the consequences of bringing in drugs. When I tell people this story, they say, "See, you can do so much more with your life. You've got a bit of intelligence." I think that comes from the family that raised me for my first fifteen years. They are well educated and well mannered.

After coming back from Jamaica, I sold crack out of my room above the bar in the Coxwell and Danforth area. I literally had people lined up down the hall, on the roof, and on the back stairs waiting to buy crack. I sold two ounces a night and drank five, six, or seven 1.8 litre bottles of Black Bull beer with 10% alcohol every day. Every single day, I drank downstairs at the bar, smoked cigarettes, ate food, and smoked at least a quarter-ounce of crack for free.

To me, it was heaven.

Then I decided to try the Detox Centre at Donlands and Danforth, just to clear my mind and get my strength together.

It ended up being one of those places where there was hope. But I didn't want hope. I wanted a vacation from partying, like people who work all week then spend their weekends up north. I wanted to party for a month or two, and then take a few days off at the Detox Centre to get some rest. That's really messed up.

When I came out of detox, things got really bad again. My mother's research led her to take me to the Renaissance Rehabilitation Program in Brooklin, Ontario, where I completed their 28-day residential program. It was my third stint in a rehab program. I completed the program and then went to Bolton with one of the other residents. He let me live at his place with his family and got me a job as a painter in a car dealership.

For a while, I worked, made money, went to Alcoholics Anonymous meetings and stayed clean. It was good.

After a few months, that job ended, so back to the city I went.

Chapter 15

STUCK IN ANTIGUA

My life continued on the same self-destructive path. I filled my days doing absolutely nothing except smoking crack, shooting dope and drinking booze. Eventually, the happy days turned into the sad days. Back then the sad days consisted of no money and no dope. I was only 23.

Lucky for me an opportunity arose once again for a magical, free vacation to Antigua. I couldn't say no, although all sorts of things started to go wrong. Before I left Toronto my contact gave me scuba gear and sent me for a scuba diving lesson. Then they paid for me to fly down to Antigua to spend a week in an all-inclusive resort where I had a great time.

The drug pick-up was supposed to be done in a different way - through scuba gear and all sorts of nonsense. When I got down there I was told to pass the scuba gear to a local contact. It must have been thousands of dollars worth of equipment. I was told to wait for the guy to bring the stuff back to me with everything all ready to go.

When the day came for my return flight to Canada my

buddy said he still needed a couple of days. Well, how the hell was I supposed to get a couple of more days when my plane ticket was already booked, pre-paid, and non-refundable.

Since I'd done this enough times before, a voice in my head told me, you're not comfortable; abandon it; don't hesitate or you're asking for trouble. I was already in too deep and felt a little bit of pressure.

My parents didn't know I was gone. They still thought I was in Toronto. Nobody knew I was out of Canada. There I was with no money, doing this for somebody different who I didn't know. I had no way of getting in touch with my Toronto contact and I was relying on this guy in Antigua, who I'd seen twice in my life, to come through with accommodation, food, money and another ticket back home.

Foolishly, I agreed to stay. He came and picked me up from the resort and dropped me off on a side street in downtown Antigua - not the most luxurious place to go. I had to walk down an alley all the way to the back and up the stairwell to a room above a grocery store. You can imagine the type of stores. People were throwing their garbage out in the alley every day, in the heat and the sun, so every time you're walking through there, hundreds of flies are zooming all over. It was disgusting.

The local guy obviously wasn't swimming in cash, because it was all being funded by the people back in Canada and he was finding it hard to scrape up enough cash for me to spend my nights in that room. It kind of reminded me of a worn down Hotel Waverly in downtown Toronto. For four or five days I stayed there, with him giving me barely enough money to eat, never mind money to enjoy myself.

With no money to get back to Toronto, I felt like a prisoner in Antigua. I didn't have even one dollar in my pocket, no phone card, no health insurance, and no plane ticket home. Basically, I was living with the hope that guy was going to come every day. I had no way of getting in touch with him. He would just show up.

One day he didn't even show up. Thank God the owner of the supermarket was a nice guy and allowed me to stay there for the night, or I would have been out on the street in Antigua, which wouldn't have been a pleasant experience. By the third day, my local contact wouldn't even stop in to see me. He'd just stop by, pay the owner of the supermarket, leave me the equivalent of ten dollars Canadian for the day, and split.

I was getting pissed off and annoyed, figuring that if I'm going to be doing this for these guys, at least they should make me feel comfortable. I wasn't expecting to be treated like a prince but I expected to be in a half decent hotel room with a couple of hundred bucks in my pocket. I didn't expect to be living in Antigua in even worse shape than I had been living back home in Toronto.

On my first day in that room, I forgot how much their money was really worth. I bought six beers and I figured I'd have a lot of money left over. Basically, the money covered six beers, a bag of chips and a chocolate bar for the whole day, but, I was an alcoholic and needed my booze. Without it, I would have gone into withdrawal and had the DT's while stuck in a rundown room in a strange country, not knowing anybody.

I ended up calling my friend Liza's father back in Toronto. (the one who sent us to the Dominican Republic on vacation.) I figured that he might be able to send me a couple of dollars to help me out. He wired me forty dollars by Western Union. I had $40.00 in my pocket and I actually went to a tourist restaurant downtown. It cost me ten or fifteen dollars to eat, but at least I got a good meal, sat around decent people, and felt a little bit better.

I ended up there for almost an extra week. Finally, I just got so worried. The guy said, "Don't worry. Tomorrow I'm going to come and get you. We've got the plane ticket already."

He wanted me to fly to a different island to meet up with somebody else. I didn't know if buddy was going to be there. I didn't know if he was sending me on a wild goose chase. Things just did not seem good at all.

I mean, think about it logically. There I was, a tourist, coming down with all this scuba gear, leaving an all-inclusive resort. Next thing you know, I miss my flight. Two weeks later, I fly from Antigua to another island with this scuba gear and then eventually fly back to Toronto. What was that going to look like at Canadian Customs?

That's when I finally thought to myself, "You know what? I may be dumb, I may be fucked up, but I'm not completely and utterly stupid".

Finally, I called my family and I told them where I was, that I was on vacation with a friend, that I had fallen in my hotel, hurt my back, went to a doctor, and missed my plane. My mom was pissed. Basically, the only help they agreed to give me was sending me enough money by Western Union to get to the Antigua airport. They found a seat for that day on a plane flying to Toronto and they paid one thousand dollars for the ticket at their end. They sent me enough money through Western Union to get a cab to the Antigua airport. I guess they called ahead and found out how much a cab was, plus, enough for departure tax. They told me that if I was on that plane, fine, but, if I wasn't - that was it, I was on my own.

The worst part about the whole ordeal was that coming back from Western Union, I went back to the grocery store to buy a beer and the owner said to me that my friend had just called and he was going to be there in half an hour to take me to the airport.

I thought to myself, "I've got to try and get all my stuff together and get out of here before this guy shows up, because if this guy shows up, I'm in a foreign country. You never know what's going to happen."

The last thing I wanted was to get killed. It would have been safer facing that dilemma in Toronto, where I knew people and people knew me. It was a little bit different being on some foreign island; I didn't want any sort of Mexican travesty.

So I grabbed my stuff, went outside and jumped into a taxi to the airport. At the airport, I pick up my ticket. It turned out that my departure tax was already included in the price of the ticket, so I had a couple of bucks extra for beer. Obviously, being an alcoholic, that came first.

There I was sitting in the bar when it suddenly dawned on me that buddy had planned to pick me up within half an hour after I left the room. I figured that my flight to another island had to be roughly close to the same time as the flight to Toronto. If buddy heard from the owner that I was gone with all my stuff, he would come to the airport looking for me.

If you have been to the Antigua airport, you would know that it's not too big. So, there I was pretending like nothing was wrong, sitting behind a post in the bar and trying not to peek around while drinking my beer. I can tell you, I was so relieved to get on that plane and get out of that country! It was a close call, but thank God, finally, I got back to Toronto.

It turned out to be not so great after all, because when

I got off the plane at the Toronto airport, the police picked me up coming off the airplane. It turned out that I had an outstanding warrant for a *'Failure to Comply with Probation'* for some minor offence.

My parents had arranged for my sister and her boyfriend to pick me up at the airport. When they discovered that I was arrested, my sister picked up my suitcase and took it to my parent's place. I ended up in jail for two weeks.

It's a damn good thing that I didn't bring that scuba stuff back with me.

Chapter 16

ALL GOOD THINGS END

After I got out of jail, I went right back to my place in the East end and started the same old trip all over again - beer, dope, girls, hanging out, doing nothing but causing trouble and wasting my life.

Things were okay for a while. People came to my room wanting drugs. I would get them their drugs and then I would get high for free. I was talking to some of my friends about what happened, and they were laughing and I was laughing.

The bottom line, as far as I was concerned, was that I was still owed some money because I went to Antigua. I had done everything that I was supposed to do. I had even stayed longer than I was supposed to, despite not knowing what the hell was going on. My Toronto contacts didn't want to give me anything, and they didn't. You know what? I said it's better to cut my ties, than to cause a situation where bad stuff could happen.

As the days went on, I ran into the friends who sent me on my first trips and I told them what was going on. They mentioned that something might be coming up going to Jamaica again. Sure enough, I jumped on it. A few weeks later, off I went to Jamaica. It's an amazing country. I wish I had gone there on a legitimate vacation.

Because of the type of life I was living, I would have loved to have stayed in Jamaica. I've come to realize that I'm not a greedy person. I want the best that I can afford, within my means and not beyond, and I'm happy with what I have, not with what I want. In that country, it was laidback. When everybody worked, they took their time, didn't work when it was too hot, worked in the morning and in the early evening, and that's it. There was a good community and it was just a slower pace. I could have handled it.

Anyway, I met these new people in Jamaica, through my Toronto contact, but the job was for somebody different and they were moving the drugs in a different way. I called back to Canada and talked to my friend who reassured me that the new people were pretty trustworthy.

My friend told me, "Take a look at it, if you like it go for it, if you don't, don't do it."

My friend in Toronto seemed to be worried about my welfare more than the money. To me that was kind of important. People do things for their own reasons - family, kids, whatever - and not all people are in it to destroy other people.

My contact told me the same thing, "If you don't like it, if you don't feel comfortable don't do it. Don't get yourself in trouble. Don't take the risk and don't take the chance if you don't think you're going to be able to make it."

I had second thoughts, but I went through with it anyway, even though I was thinking that I didn't want to do it for any money. I should have followed my instincts, because, like they say, all good things come to an end. And they sure did.

Let's just say that was my last trip. I flew back to Toronto and while I was in the customs line I had this feeling that something wasn't right. They pulled me over and just the way they did it, it seemed like they had been waiting for me.

I think what might have happened is that I might not have been a mule, but a decoy. I think that sometimes when you leave a destination like Jamaica, or any of the islands, other people are trying to move drugs at the same time. Sometimes, there are five or six people on a plane doing it, sometimes none, sometimes there's only one. I don't know who it is that's doing it; I'm just thinking that's a possibility.

My theory is that, in the islands, they watch the airports and the departures and the people who are lining up to get their tickets. Then they'll look at people and try to pick out who looks more likely to do something like that and who doesn't. Then, just after the plane leaves the island, they'll call the destination country and describe the people to look out for. When the plane lands, Customs Officers are waiting for these two people who are arriving and they search them.

When the Customs Officers are directed to those people, other people slip through a lot easier. I think that's what happened with me.

I could see them looking at me from a distance, even before I got to the front of the line. They were glancing up, glancing down, looking at their notepads. Anyway, I went down.

I was caught with 2.28 kilos of cocaine strapped to my legs. They got me at the airport in Toronto. They let me call my lawyer; I used the same lawyer all the time. All my lawyer said to me was, "You're fucked now!" Yep, I knew that. I mean, how can you not be fucked when you're found like that?

So they questioned me, tried to get me to say blah, blah, blah who was I doing it for blah, blah, blah. My story was always that I was doing it for myself. I figured I'd make some quick cash. I heard about it through the grapevine. That was my story and that's what I was sticking to.

Also, my lawyer mentioned just to keep saying over and over again, "By the advice of my attorney, I'm using my right to remain silent."

From the airport, I was taken to a Peel Police Station to spend the night. That was the first time I was in a police station where they actually gave me a McDonald's breakfast. I was going, "Holy smoke! In Toronto, you're lucky if you even get a cup of coffee."

Then, the lunch at court was also hot McDonald's! I mean you go down to the College Park, Queen's Park, or Old City Hall Courts in Toronto and see what kind of lunch you get. You're lucky if you get stale cheese sandwiches. The last time I was down there the choice was either half-frozen cheese sandwiches, or half-frozen tuna sandwiches on a stale bun with one glass of juice.

That's why a lot of people, especially people who are in and out of jail all the time, prefer not to go to court. Or they like to do video-court, or spread out their court dates as much as possible.

Going to court is risky. You're getting out of jail for a few hours. You're moving around. You're seeing other people and there is more potential for violence. Not only that, the food sucks and nobody wants to go and lose their hot meal. Everyone would rather stay in jail and eat a hot meal, even though they're not too appetizing. But they're a lot better than a half-frozen tuna sandwich.

Chapter 17

WAITING FOR TRIAL

From the Peel jail, they sent me to Maplehurst Institution for a couple of months. From there they took me back and forth to court at College Park in Toronto.

Maplehurst is a one level jail with both a Correctional Centre and a Detention Centre. You stay in the Detention Centre while you're going to court. Once you're sentenced, they ship you to a different institution which has a Correctional Centre. Maplehurst had both sides. That was before they built the "super jails".

There I was, going back and forth to court for a couple of months, meeting different people, some interesting, some not, and I got to learn a lot about people.

Some of the people you couldn't believe were even in jail. Some of them didn't even look like they could commit a crime. They were old, out of shape, could barely walk and some could barely breathe. There were also some really scary people. There again, I drew on my adaptability skills. I'm pretty good at that.

It wasn't that bad. Back then you could still smoke inside, so you could order up to two cartons of cigarettes and a bail of tobacco from the canteen every week or two. I still had my smoking.

Then all of a sudden, I was the person who had been there the longest - two or three months. My lawyer would get me court dates as far apart as possible, because I was doing time regardless. I figured the more dead time I did, the more my sentence would be reduced.

They were about to build the new super jail and anybody who had court dates longer than two weeks between each appearance got shipped out. For a while, it was like Russian roulette, different names were called and you were praying that it wasn't you because you didn't want to go somewhere else.

I'd been in my range the longest. I was serving the food. I was cleaning. I was out of my cell longer than everybody else. I got to use the phone longer and I got more meals. Sometimes I was eating two or three extra meals at a time. I was living life, and to be honest, I was enjoying it. It was a lot better than fighting, robbing, getting robbed, smoking crack and drinking beer all day.

I mean, hanging around with people is what you do on the outside, but inside, there is a sense of unity among certain people, which is kind of a good thing. It's the us-against-them mentality.

I was lucky to get shipped to the old Wellington bucket, which is on the same property as Guelph Correctional Facility. It was a smaller detention jail that was more like a retreat. There were only ten people on a range. In some other jails there were thirty to forty people on a range.

The problem with the Wellington Institution was that it

was one of the first ones with a No Smoking Policy.

For me, with my smoking addiction, going from an institution where you were still allowed to buy a full canteen's worth of tobacco, to a jail where you couldn't smoke anything, was a big problem.

Obviously, I had nothing else to do but smoke, play chess, checkers, cards, and walk around in the yard. So that sucked. For those of us who knew what was happening, we did manage to sneak some tobacco with us from Maplehurst.

When it was time to leave, they called your name to come to the front. Then they would lock you in the *bubble*. Then they walked you back to your cell to make sure you got everything, so you couldn't get any packages ready to bring drugs with you.

Any of us who heard "Come to the bubble after lunch" got our packages ready in advance. I think I brought two bails of tobacco with me. Another guy I was with brought two bails with him.

We figured we were pretty golden. Anyway, when we got there, they were very lax with checking. We had the tobacco "suitcased", so to speak ... Use your imagination.

We managed to be able to get on the same range and in the same cell.

Sometimes at night the cops would walk by doing their rounds, and we would hear them saying, "Haven't you two run out of tobacco yet?" Twice a day they brought you popcorn to try and stop the urges. They also had Nicorettes on the canteen list, but it was really expensive, much more than what they were charging for a carton of cigarettes. I was on the same range the whole time I was at Wellington and got more time under my belt.

Until this point, I was doing my time in provincial jails waiting to have my trial. Unfortunately, importing drugs is a federal offence and once you get sentenced, you go to a federal penitentiary.

The prosecution was threatening to give me eight to twelve years for importing drugs. They said they would reduce the sentence if I pleaded guilty. I don't know if that was just a scare tactic, or if they were hoping for a quick guilty plea.

When they took me to court for my trial, I agreed to plead guilty and that day got sentenced to 38 months. The downfall was that I was thinking they were asking for all that time, but since I had already served time waiting for sentencing, I had calculated that I had already done "X" months, times two, and they would take the time served right off my sentence. That didn't quite happen the way I thought it would.

I didn't want to get sentenced. I wanted to wait for another canteen because when you go to Millhaven, you're only allowed a thirty dollar loan and that usually has to last you for two or three weeks. That's really not much if you think about it - especially when you're in Millhaven, where you're locked up for twenty-two hours a day while you are going through the assessment unit. If you the hit general population side and you refuse to work, it's the same sort of thing.

Chapter 18

DOING TIME

First I was taken from Maplehurst, and then to the East Detention Centre to spend one night. The next day I was put on the Big Goose, a Grey Coach bus with boxes for the protective custody people. We were shackled and handcuffed.

When the bus pulled up to Millhaven and I saw the gun towers and the big concrete walls, and we entered, everything felt like a penitentiary.

Reality struck. The feeling was a lot different than just a regular jail.

They took the general population guys out first into a big cage and then they took the protective custody (P.C.) guys out and put them in the same cage. Half of them must have probably shit themselves because they thought that they were going to be safe for their whole trip. What they didn't realize is that in the penitentiary, in the federal system, it's all integrated meaning that the P.C.s are with the general population, unless you're deemed a "maximum offender" - meaning that you're a serial rapist, murderer, or child killer. They go to Kingston

Penitentiary and regular dangerous people go to Millhaven.

For the first little while I refused to work and was still really anti-authoritarian. I had a heavy-duty chip on my shoulder. Finally, I realized that if I worked, I could walk around to more areas, get a lot more exercise, and eat better food.

In the federal prison, everything was run differently. You were allowed articles in your cell like a TV, a radio, some tapes, video games, and a certain number of T-shirts.

The people I used to take trips for made sure that I had a TV and made sure that my canteen had money. You can never judge a person by what they do. Most people think, "Oh, drug dealers They don't care about nobody and, blah, blah, blah." But some people have a heart and they're just doing what they can to survive.

People ask, "How can you become more addicted when you're inside?" Well I did. Drugs are everywhere in every institution from Millhaven to any other institution. There are all the drugs that you want. It's just a little bit more expensive. In Millhaven you're paying $100 for a point, which is a tenth of a gram.

When you work your way down to minimum security jails - Frontenac or Beavercreek - it's only fifty dollars for a point because you are closer to the street. If you're used to paying $100 a point and then all of a sudden it's only $50 - that's two for one.

Thanks to my friends, I was never without canteen money. Three cartons of cigarettes traded for a point and I think I was paying $15 a carton because you don't pay taxes in a federal institution.

With three cartons of Export A Green, I was wheeling and dealing. I was up to smoking roughly two packs of cigarettes a day and I was usually going through a big tin of tobacco and two cartons of cigarettes every canteen period.

In Millhaven, when you're stuck in a cell for so long and all you have is TV, at first you think it's great. You do nothing. You can just lie around and watch TV, or try to read a book. But being confined is like living in your washroom for a week. Try it and you'll experience how some people feel. Then imagine doing it for a couple of years.

So, with an opiate addiction, it makes you relax, you go on the nod, you're passing in and out of consciousness, and time goes by a little bit faster - a little bit easier. That's why a lot of people who come out of jail after doing long stretches of time are opiate addicts.

When they get out, imagine them trying to deal with the public. I mean, in prison it's orderly. Everything is run a certain way. Then, all of a sudden you go from a controlled environment where you walk down the hallway on one side of the hall and don't look into anybody's cell. Then, suddenly you are outside and going onto the TTC subway at rush hour and open to confrontation. It gets so frustrating that your head just wants to explode.

That's what happens with a lot of people. I think they re-offend because they don't know how to function on the outside. The only thing they know how to do is commit a crime. Most guys have no money when they get out. They go back to their home, or they have enough to pay for a place to sleep for the night at a hotel, or they put down enough money for a month for a room.

What's the worst that's going to happen? They're going to end up back in jail with a roof over their heads and food. So they have a good time and party their hearts out. Some of them just go on a binge and rob, steal, hurt, and just do as much drugs and booze as possible. They just do what they want and then the worst thing that happens is that they get arrested. They get a five-year sentence and they're out in three. I'm not saying that's good. That's how some people think!

After several months in Millhaven, I was going for parole and was sent down to Frontenac - a minimum security prison. It didn't have any surrounding walls or gates and you could work on their farm and walk around the property.

Eventually, I was paroled to a halfway house in downtown Toronto. I wasn't even there a month and some guy didn't return one day. He phoned in and said the reason he didn't come back was because they had me there. He told them that I was selling him and the other guys in the halfway house drugs - cocaine to be exact - and how could he stay there and stay clean if they had a dealer in the house?

To make a long story short, they questioned me, questioned me, and questioned me a whole bunch of times.

The next thing I knew, the police were there to arrest me and they were revoking my parole for suspicion. They had no proof. They were just going by this guy's word, so that obviously proves that he's a pretty promising informant - meaning he informed a lot. He was a rat and I suppose his information was usually reliable.

Unfortunately, this time I didn't do it. I figured the first warning is free, the second one they send you to the bucket for two or three days, and then they'll bring you back out. The third time they might or might not let you back out. Me, I got sent back right away. No second chances for me.

So, you have a chance of signing your waiver, which means you sign off on your parole hearing and you go right back to your institution. I said to myself, you've got to be kidding me! Some guy runs away from the halfway house, calls in and tells them this. They find no cocaine; there is nobody else that says I did anything. How can they not let me out?

Well, sure enough, they denied me parole, saying the facts were too "bright" or whatever. Anyway, it just so happened that this same idiot happened to be somebody who was in the Frontenac Institution when I was there. He owed the Italians so much money that he had to give up his TV and all his canteens for basically his whole stay. I would feed him with cigarettes, give him my ice cream. I would let him into my house to watch my TV when I went to work, because by that time I was working at Frontenac.

The reason I helped him out like that was because he was hanging around with people that I knew from another institution. So you figure, if you're hanging around with certain people from another institution who are okay, the people that they know must be okay.

Sure enough, he happens to be the same person who makes me do the last two years of my sentence.

Chapter 19

MEETING BRITTANY

I was sent back to Beaver Creek, outside Gravenhurst, for the rest of my sentence, where I met a girl named Brittany through another inmate. He was a good-hearted friend. He was not very experienced in life. He just happened to do a stupid thing without thinking of the consequences and was convicted for an offence without actually committing the violence. In real life, he wouldn't hurt a fly and he would do anything for people.

He introduced me to his friend Brittany, when she came to see him one Visitor's Day. They were good friends. After that, she started to visit me almost every week. We were getting along so well that she started coming up twice a week to visit. She was a great girl and we were having so much fun. She was really good for me.

After a few more months, the time came for me to try for another parole. They gave me the option of either trying for a parole or applying for a Temporary Absence Program (TAP) which would allow me a temporary leave of 72 hours once a month.

My parole officer and I discussed my history and what had happened on my previous parole. I decided that my best option would be to go for the temporary passes because she didn't think I would make parole. I guess your previous record speaks volumes later on in life.

On my passes, Brittany would drive up from the city and pick me up. We'd go and get drunk; we'd party, and it was going along really good. She was there picking me up every month. We would spend the weekend together and then she would drive me back to the institution.

I was lucky. I had a girlfriend who loved me.

When I finally got released, I was sent to a halfway house near Hamilton and from there I worked in a pallet factory, driving a forklift every day for sixty days. I got my forklift certificate. It was a neat program.

Brittany and I kept dating and things were going good. When the forklift program was finished, I moved back to Toronto to my parents' place for a while and found a forklift job in a warehouse where I made good money. I worked at a couple of different jobs throughout my relationship with Brittany.

I loved Brittany. I gave her my heart and she still has it. I met her family and she met mine. She loved my grandparents and my grandparents loved her. My mom loved her and so did my dad. After a few months, we got engaged and we were going to get married.

One May, we went camping in the mountains of British Columbia. We went to Burnaby and stayed at Harrison Hot Springs. It was a romantic get-away. We loved to camp. We used to go camping every long weekend. That was the first time I'd ever left the province with anyone in a dating relationship.

I think we made a lot of mistakes by spending a lot of money and pushing our limits, just so that we could be accepted into a circle where everyone else was living by stature - that is, based on how much money they made. Instead of having dinner at the Keg, it had to be someplace posh, with an Italian name. It was never Coffee Time. It had to be Starbucks.

I wasn't a completely changed man. I mean I was good in my way. I was nice to her. I never physically hurt her or anything like that. But I wasn't this changed guy just because things were going well. There were still nights when I was smoking crack behind her back.

After six months, it got to the point where I was holding a job and was just able to squeak by on the higher lifestyle that she wanted. We both maxed out our bank overdrafts every pay period. I was clearing almost one thousand dollars every two weeks and there I was at my five hundred dollar overdraft limit. That money wasn't spent on drugs. That was for going out with Brittany for dinners - having an entrée and a bottle of wine and spending $100.

I couldn't keep up with the lifestyle she wanted. I'm happy with the necessities of life and a little bit more. She was only happy if she had everything. I mean it's good to dream and strive for things. You've got to work together and forge goals - not just say *this is what I want and if you can't provide it, see you later.*

I don't think she realized that the way most people afforded those things was that they saved and they waited. They lived within their means, not above their means.

Things just kind of went south because we had a lot of debts. It was a relationship with lots of ups and downs. It came to the point where I would fight with her in order to be alone for the weekend, so I could smoke crack, or get some cocaine and do some pills without her knowing.

We split up after almost two years. That was a few years ago and I just haven't been able to feel the same feelings with anyone else that I felt for her. Even now, I still have strong feelings for her. Since then, I've dated and had fun, but since Brittany I have never known someone who I thought I could actually settle down with.

As I said, I gave Brittany my heart and I don't want it back. She's got it and that's what I thought when we broke up. There's no one else who can replace her. I even think if she came back today and we talked and we decided to try again, I would love her just as much, if not more than I did when we were together at our happiest moments. That's what I mean by her having my heart.

She was the one I was going to marry. Even now I think she is, or could possibly be, the woman that I am supposed to spend the rest of my life with. But I realize that just because I feel that way about her, it doesn't mean that she could feel that way about me, or that she could want to spend the rest of her life with me.

If we tried again today - if I saw her today and she said "Let's see where this goes." - the love that I still have for her would have to be the same sort of love she gives back.

That's how I would know that we were both meant to be together for the rest of our lives.

Chapter 20

DOWNHILL AGAIN

When Brittany and I broke up, I was still living at home with my parents, but they were fed up with me. I lost my job. I stopped contributing to the rent and became belligerent. I was an adult, yet I argued about everything and continued to try to manipulate my parents. Finally, they told me to get help or leave. I left.

Once again, I moved back upstairs at the bar at Coxwell and Danforth. I quickly returned to my old routine of crack, heroin, booze and women. Almost five years had passed since my arrest and I was right back to where I had started. It was as if I had never left.

There were a few different people hanging around, but some of the regulars were still there and some started to come back, like it happens with any sort of social circle. The way it gets bigger is that you know somebody who starts hanging around. You start talking to them. Then they start talking to some-body else. Next thing you know, they're also in the circle of friends.

That's what happened with a guy I knew a while back. I'd only met Marco a handful of times and I guess he started hanging around more and more. He was coming to my room to buy crack. He was messed up. He was one of those full-fledged party guys. He partied until his body shut down - like I used to do on a periodic basis. He was doing that on a regular basis and would get a little crazy and a little psychotic and do stupid things that he wouldn't remember.

One day my friend Charity and I were in my room selling crack. This Marco shows up with a whole bag full of change and about a dozen new ties that he had stolen. He was looking them over in my room and tried to sell them to Charity. She said, "What would I do with dress ties? I don't have a man in my life."

Marco was one of those guys who, after he was around for a while, you didn't want him there, whether he took drugs or not. You would be relieved and there was a weight lifted off your head after he had gone.

Charity was ready to leave and as she was going out the door she said, "I'll see you tomorrow."

She almost didn't.

After she left, Marco was so messed up that he accused her of stealing one of his ties. Just as he said that, she came back upstairs because she had forgotten something. Again, he asked her if she had seen the missing tie. Again, she said no.

She stayed there with me. I let Marco go through my whole room, tear up my mattress, go through my cupboards Just because he's one of those crazy guys, you want him to clear his mind and get the fuck out of your house. Of course he didn't find the tie.

The next thing you know he's going, "Oh she body-packed

it, she body packed it."

Marco assumed that Charity shoved it down her pants or put it in her underwear, which is kind of ridiculous because she didn't need to steal. If she wanted something, she could have afforded to buy it.

All of a sudden, it turned into a big conspiracy that me and this girl had set up before he showed up. Think about that - I had no clue he was coming over - how was it possible that me and this girl could have conspired beforehand and made a plan in order to steal a tie? It was crazy and so was he.

Eventually, he ran out of my room and down the fire escape outside my open window.

I was at the top of the fire escape and he was in the alley below freaking out. So I went down to confront him. I guess my size intimidated him. He took off down the back alley. Marco always told everybody that he was an ex-enforcer for a biker gang in Toronto, so I figured that if his story was true, he was tough.

All he said, as he was rounding the corner onto Coxwell, was, "I'll be back tomorrow and then you won't be laughing."

You know, he was my acquaintance/friend and I knew he got a little crazy after he'd been up for a few days doing pills and methadone and all sorts of nonsense. I was pretty sure that once he got some sleep, Marco would wake up and say something like, "Oh fuck, I must have made an ass of myself. I'm sorry."

So that's what I figured would happen. I didn't see him the next day. I figured okay, good, he's sleeping. He'll sleep for a couple of days and then he'll be back and either apologize or just not say anything. I really wasn't expecting an apology, I just wanted him to show up to make sure that the situation was over. Bikers were known for their attitude - *when a man says he's going to do something, a man means it.*

Anyways, I'd been up for about three days and still no sign of him. I was getting tired and drunker because I'd been drinking for three days and smoking crack.

I remember it was somewhere between eight and nine in the morning and I finally said, "Fuck this. I'm going to bed.

Then I shut my window, locked it, locked my door, and climbed into bed.

Chapter 21

NEAR DEATH

The next thing I remembered was a sharp pain pulling from my stomach. My eyes opened and I saw Marco pulling a knife out of my stomach.

I was on my side in bed and I rolled onto my back. I donkey-kicked him in the chest and he flew up against the wall and then stumbled backwards towards my window. Somehow, I got up and into a defensive stance.

I said, "What's your fucking problem?"

Marco said, "How could you do that? How could you steal from me? How you could let someone steal from me? I thought we were friends."

I said, "Bud, you should know me better than that. There is no fucking way I would let anyone steal from anyone in my house, let alone from someone that I know."

Marco stood there for a second and said, "Oh shit, I think I made a mistake!"

"You're damn right you made a mistake."

Then Marco said, "Can we talk about this?"

"We'll talk about this when I come back from the hospital," I answered.

Marco should have just realized that enough was enough. Instead, what did he do? He picked up my cell phone like an idiot and called everybody, including the owner of the bar where I lived. He said, "I'm the one that just tried to kill Dan and if he doesn't die at the hospital, I'm going to sneak in there dressed as a doctor and finish the job."

Of course I didn't know anything about this at the time. My mother told me this later. All I remember is being in excruciating pain, finding my way down the stairs to the street and stumbling up Coxwell towards the hospital, while clutching my hand to my bleeding stomach.

Cabbies wouldn't stop. Nobody would stop for me - I guess because I was dirty, covered in blood, no shoes, no shirt, and just shorts on. My blood was everywhere. People didn't want to stop.

Lucky for me a very kind Portuguese lady stopped her car, picked me up and drove me to Emergency at the hospital. It turned out that she worked there as a cleaner.

All I remember after that was hearing my own voice screaming and yelling at the nurses and at my mom. I remember my mom trying to talk to me and then telling me that I was being rude and I should let the nurses help me.

I was just in so much pain. They did a CAT scan and I needed emergency surgery. I guess they had to first wait for the pain medication that they had given me earlier to wear off.

They thought my bowels were filling up with blood. They were afraid the knife might have pierced my bowel, so I signed the consent form for surgery. I remember the doctor telling me, just before he put me out, that people with this sort of injury, going into this sort of surgery, might have to have - he was just warning me - might have to have a colostomy bag.

At that point I was conscious and all I wanted him to do was put me out. Why would I be worrying about a colostomy bag when I was basically dying?

Then I was rushed into the surgery.

I remember the first face that I saw when I woke up was the face of the girl I was supposed to marry. Brittany was standing next to my bed, right next to my mother and father. I think my mother must have called her. At the time, I wanted Brittany to stay longer and talk, but the next thing I knew, I passed right back out.

I didn't wake up until the next day. There was a morphine drip in me and I had fifty staples in my stomach. When I woke up there was no colostomy bag, thank God, but I had a catheter [ouch].

The next day I woke up and there was an armed security guard at my door. I was wondering, *what the hell is this for?* It turned out that a security guard was outside my door for the entire eight days that I was in the hospital. That was because of the phone calls that idiot Marco had made, threatening to sneak into the hospital dressed as a doctor and kill me.

Marco never got arrested. When the police questioned me, I told them I didn't know anything. I wasn't going to rat out Marco.

My mother stayed in my hospital room with me every day during the week I was there. She was trying to convince me to get help, but I argued with her all the time. She wanted me to go straight to a rehab program after the hospital. I said nothing was wrong with me.

To show you how really stupid I was back then, not really giving a shit about anything, including myself, I basically rushed my way out of the hospital. I had some money in my pocket to go downstairs to buy cigarettes at the store. I convinced the doctors to let me go and that I was going to be okay. So, before they decided to let me out, I went downstairs and hopped in a cab.

All I wanted to do was get back to my room over the bar. The police seal was still on my door, from the day I got stabbed. The first thing I wanted to do was smoke crack, but Charity, the person that sold me crack, wouldn't let me. She wouldn't sell me crack and didn't want to see me smoking crack until my stitches and staples were gone.

She actually stayed for an hour and half in that mangy little room and scrubbed everything down with bleach, including my window, my walls, and my floor.

Then she went out and bought me new pillows, new linens and a comforter. That's when I realized Charity was more than just my drug dealer, she was my friend. Basically, she was the only friend I had.

So there I was sneaking out and buying dope from someone else, getting high, and having my steroid inhalers and stuff to help me heal. I was still so stupid. Not only did I move back to the same place, I moved back into the same room and I was still taking afternoon naps with my door wide open. Obviously Marco hadn't been caught and he might have come back.

By that time, I was thinking that the guy had to realize that I wasn't going to do anything to him or rat on him. So just forget the whole situation and just move on.

You would think that if anything would have scared me straight, that stabbing would have done the trick. Almost being killed in your sleep is scary enough to make you want to quit everything and go back to eating baby food.

For most people, that would have been a life-altering event. Not for me. If anything, it immersed me deeper into the drug culture. More people wanted to share their dope with me, wanted to hang out with me, and looked up to me. People would say, "Oh, there's Dan, he's the one that got stabbed." Not only was I the story over a beer downstairs at the bar, but they also built me up to be a good guy who survived something bad and wasn't afraid.

Chapter 22

CRY FOR HELP - DETOX

One of the waitresses at the bar was living in a house at Woodbine, right across the street from the subway. I hadn't planned to move in with her. I just wanted to get away from the bar for a few days. Next thing you know, my landlord at the bar doesn't think I'm coming back. Since it was the end of the month, he decided to move someone else into my room. So I just started selling crack out of her place.

There were only two apartments in that house, the main floor and the basement. The house was in an area that wasn't busy like the bar, where there had been sixty people lined up down the hall, or coming up and down the fire escape. People weren't knocking on the windows, or smoking crack in the bathroom and the hallway, like they were at the bar. Not long after I moved in, I moved out.

I signed into Detox once again, as a last resort. I was hoping maybe I'd have an eye-opening experience. I did want to stop, but I guess my heart wasn't in it. My desire and my strength to stay clean weren't there. I mean, if it happened, it happened if it didn't, it didn't. That was my mentality. When you're still feeling like that, there's no way you're even close to ready. Other people might see you as ready, and can't believe that you're still alive, considering the way you look and the stories that you tell.

There were many times when I walked through the door at that Detox Centre. I gained a rapport with the people who worked there and they truly cared about me. This time, one of the counsellors gave me a shock of reality, "Oh, my God, Dan, I can't believe you're still alive. Look at you! You look horrible."

The counsellors were there to help you and not to judge. They told you the truth and told you exactly what they saw.

I remember we were in the night group and we were all expressing how our day went and talking about our hopes for the future, and that sort of thing. One of the counsellors interrupted and said, "Excuse me, I don't mean to be too personal, but we have a relationship with Dan, so I'm going to be kind of blunt."

He looked right at me and he said, "Look at you. What the hell are you doing? You look horrible. You look disgusting, like the walking dead."

I was, 6'3" and 140 lbs., malnourished with black underneath my eyes from lack of sleep. My collar bones were like soup bowls and I hadn't really noticed. I thought I looked good. I thought I was fit. Suddenly, I realized I was wasting away.

He said, "You're killing yourself. If you go back out there and use, you're going to die."

Tears came to my eyes without shame because his words had hit home. Deep down inside I knew that it was true. I just didn't want to face the facts.

I was only there for a week before I snuck in some dope and I was doing it with a couple of other people. I was brought in for a urinalysis and they threw me out.

I went there for help because it was time to clean myself up. Instead, I had been thrown right back into the street; my mistake, my problem and I deserved it.

Sure, I was jeopardizing everybody else there by using. I mean everybody was very vulnerable. They had families and they were trying to restore their lives, which I wasn't ready to do, obviously. So, I can't really blame the people for kicking me out, even though I resented them at the time.

I had nowhere to go. I didn't know what I was going to do. I was hurting bad and I thought, "Great, here I go again."

Then I called my father. He told me that I needed serious help and that it was time to check into a long-term rehabilitation program. I knew that I would have to make the call myself, because I was an adult.

I begged my dad to pay for one night at a hotel, so I could get some sleep and think about it. He agreed to pay for one night at a cheap downtown hotel, so I could get some sleep. He refused to give me any money. Instead, he called the hotel and paid them directly.

My dad told me to call him in the morning only if I decided to check myself into a rehab centre. Otherwise, he said I shouldn't contact him again until I was ready to admit that I was an addict and needed help.

Chapter 23

HITTING BOTTOM

The next day I was thrown out of the hotel because I couldn't pay for another night. I had an option to call my father, but I didn't. I was as stubborn as always.

I didn't know what I was going to do. I had nowhere else to go. I was in an unfamiliar area of the city with only five dollars in my pocket.

I walked straight to the liquor store, bought a can of 10% beer, and then slipped a mickey of whiskey inside my jacket. For a couple of days, I panhandled to buy drugs, stole booze and food from stores, and slept for maybe one hour each night.

I knew my parents were frantic and probably not able to sleep. They didn't know where I was or what I was doing. They knew I had nowhere to live.

I was sick and tired of the life I was leading. I wasn't really a thief. I didn't want to steal or rob anybody, but that's how messed up and twisted I had become. I felt stealing was my last resort.

At the same time, I was thinking that if I got arrested, I'd go to jail for a while. That seemed almost like a retreat to me, like the detox centre. It would give me time to clear my head, get my sanity back a little bit, and figure out a plan for when I got out of jail.

As I walked around downtown, I drank a tall can of 10% beer and a mickey of whiskey. To add stupidity to stupidity, I took ten Valium pills. I really didn't know what the hell was happening.

In the middle of the afternoon, in broad daylight, I went into a convenience store, distracted the owner, grabbed money out of the till, and ran away.

I got over two hundred bucks. I was trying to put the money into my pocket, but I was wearing tear-away track pants that had no pockets and the money was falling out onto the street. There I was, trying to pick up the money, and the convenience store guy was trying to chase me down. Everybody else was yelling and screaming at me.

I ran into an alley and thought, "Fuck, I'm so messed up."

I figured that if they didn't find any money on me, then they couldn't prove I robbed the store. So I went into the back alley, rolled up the money, tied it in a piece of garbage bag and hooped it. What the hell?

Anyway, I hopped into a cab and just as we turned the corner, I saw police swarming everywhere on foot and in their cars. I was just lucky to get away. I made it back to the hotel where I had stayed before. I paid cash for the night and then went up and hid the rest of the money in the toilet tank.

In the morning, the money came out all wet and I told the guy at the front desk that the money fell in the sink when I washed my hands, which is kind of sick. It added a bit of humour to a desperate, horrible experience.

It's something I totally, totally, really regret that I ever did.

That morning, I finally called my family from a payphone. Of course, they didn't know any of this. I told them that I needed help. I was addicted to drugs and would go to rehab.

My mom said, "We will pick you up in one hour. Be at the donut shop at the corner of Bloor and Spadina. If you are there, fine, but if you don't show up, don't ever call us again, unless you are serious about getting help.

I was already at the donut shop waiting, when I remembered where I put my dope. I was thinking, "Okay, I have 3.5 grams of crack left in that hotel room and I need to get it. I ran back to the hotel, but they wouldn't let me back into the room.

It was sort of a sign from God.

Me - I tend to back out of things at the last minute. I was contemplating backing out and taking off on my parents. I was weighing the consequences of doing that.

Then I ran back to the coffee shop. I was twenty minutes late. Lucky for me, my parents were still there waiting for me in their car.

I opened the back door, threw my torn green garbage bag onto the back seat and slid in beside it. That one bag contained everything that I still owned.

My dad started driving. My mom handed me a large coffee and a paper bag with a couple of cheese bagels.

Then she said, "We won't be stopping for anything until we get to the Quebec border. We're taking you to a residential drug rehabilitation program in Quebec.

They didn't say another word to me until we got to Quebec. I was a mess. I was exhausted, hungry, and dirty. I hadn't showered for days. I slept most of the way.

We drove for almost nine hours. When we got to Trois Rivière, they told me that Narconon was the only program in Canada that would take me without me calling first and admitting that I was an addict.

It was one of those places where you pay between $18,000 and $25,000 to do the program for three or four months. My parents had to pay all the money when we arrived.

After they signed me in and paid, they left me there and drove straight back home. I can't believe the stress they must have felt.

Chapter 24

REHAB IN QUEBEC

Narconon was a little bit different than other rehabilitation or detox centres. They had a couple of hours of programming in the morning followed by free time. Then there were more programs in the afternoon, and free time for the rest of the day.

They had a sauna, TVs, video games, and basketball. It was on a huge piece of land, so it wasn't like most rehab centres where you were stuck inside.

You had a lot of time to socialize. There were a lot of people were from the States. I met people from New York, Jersey, Pittsburgh, Alabama, Kentucky, and St. Louis. Some people really wanted to be there. Some people didn't.

Like all the rehabs before, I really didn't think I needed to be there. At first they put me in the detox area to withdraw from drugs and alcohol. This guy from Pittsburgh was going through the detox with me and we both had the same, *"I don't give a shit"* attitude. That's probably why we got along so well.

All of a sudden, I realized that I was that kind of guy - an asshole with an attitude - a wannabe tough guy. It's almost like being the class clown, but causing actual harm to other people and finding it amusing.

Now that I'm thinking about it, that was pretty sick in itself. But that just goes to show you that I had no conscience and cared about absolutely nobody but myself and my drugs.

I did change my ways in the program. The staff thought that I had come a long way. After six weeks, I was put to work in the detox side, helping with the orientation for new people who were coming into detox.

Things were going well. After a couple of months, I had an opportunity to come to Toronto for one night with one of the senior staff. We were going there to pick up another guy from the Don Jail in Toronto. The court had ordered rehab for him and his parents had agreed to pay.

The counsellor and I stayed at a downtown hotel, in separate rooms. We were scheduled to pick up the new guy the next morning and then drive back.

That afternoon my parents picked me up and we went for an early dinner. I was surprised and happy when Brittany showed up at the restaurant. My parents had told her where I was and that I was doing okay. She knew I was messed up, but she had no idea about all the stuff I had been into.

After dinner, Brittany drove me back to my hotel and dropped me off. Then, I basically had free range until we were supposed to leave the next morning.

You know me. My plan was to call my contact and order drugs for some people at Narconon who wanted them. People from all different places, like Texas, were waiting for this stuff.

I knew full well that once I got back, there would be a

urinalysis test just to make sure I was still clean. That was part of the program, obviously.

Still I couldn't resist. Stupid me, when I got the drugs, I couldn't wait even one night. I had to dip in. Once I dipped in, I thought, "You know what? I might as well go all the way."

So, I ended up smoking all the drugs, not knowing how I was going to pay those guys back, but I just didn't care. I was already in the city, in my element near Jarvis and Dundas. That's where I was comfortable. That was my home. The *old me* would have run away from the situation.

This time, I didn't run. I went back to Quebec the next day. They did a urinalysis and it was dirty. Then they suspended me from the program for ten days and sent me back to the city. My parents refused to take me in.

I stayed with a friend. I didn't know what I was going to do - if I was going to go back or not. Then I realized that Narconon was sort of a world inside a world - it was a long-term program and there were people on staff that I knew and liked being around.

I knew that if I finished the program, there could be an opportunity for me to actually work there. People who finished the program could stay on and live there as volunteers if they paid rent of $400.00 a month. Then they could eventually become paid staff members. Technically, I could have started a whole new life in that program, become a counsellor and kept the program going. So that was my idea.

So, at the end of the suspension, I decided to go back and they put me in detox and assessed me and my urinalysis came back clean.

I started again. They allowed me to take the program at my own pace because of the changes they had seen from when I first arrived. From being rebellious, I had changed and started to work with new guys from the States.

I didn't really want to stop doing drugs, but that was a safe place and I was comfortable and stable.

One day a buddy asked me if I could get him some drugs. So now what I was going to do? I was going to get my contact in Toronto to send me some stuff via overnight Purolator, wrapped up in baggies, or in the bottom of a bottle of hand lotion. That way I'd get high, this guy would get high and everything would be fine.

I convinced him to get someone in his family in the States to send $200 US by Western Union to my contact in Toronto. My contact was going to send the drugs, but decided not to. Instead, my contact said he would send back the money and not get involved.

Anyway, when the drugs didn't arrive, this guy decided that I ripped him off. He knew I wanted the drugs as much as he did and I wasn't going anywhere. It wasn't like I got the money and took off. The money was in Ontario and we were in Quebec.

So buddy goes and calls his parents; then he went and told the director and all these people. They had a big talk with me and they were going to suspend me and send me home again.

I denied everything. They had no proof. His parents were furious. This guy was stupid to say anything. He was a fucking rat in my mind.

Things had been escalating and they had already talked to my parents. I knew this was going to be my downfall, so I jumped on the phone and told my parents what I was being accused of and that they were going to send me back home for 30 days.

My mom said to me on the phone, "Obviously, you haven't changed. You haven't learned anything. You're not doing anything to change. You are just doing the same things over and over again. You're just the same and this is all a lie. Don't call us again."

Then my mom hung up on me.

Well, to me that was it. In my mind, everything I had worked for to get a better relationship with my family was gone because of this guy. Instead of him waiting and being patient, he basically destroyed my life. In my mind he was to blame. I didn't have my family anymore and it was his fault.

I ran downstairs. He was in the sauna. I opened the door and he was sitting there looking at me. The next thing I knew I just ran over and soccer-ball kicked him right in the face, like I was kicking a field goal. Blood went everywhere. I was on top of him when security came. They were trying to take me off and people were screaming.

Next thing you know, I was escorted by security back to my room. The guy called his parents and his parents wanted the centre to charge me. They said they couldn't do that because they didn't know what really happened.

Later, I found out that when I kicked buddy's front teeth, he lost two teeth and one tooth went through his lip.

The next thing I know this guy's parents called the Quebec police and wanted to charge me over the phone.

One of the staff members then said, "Listen, we have to get you on the train. We've got to get you out of the province or else there are going to be big problems; either you're going to stay in jail here in Quebec for a while, where you don't know any French, or, what the police tend to do with little matters like this is, they'll actually drive you to the border and leave you there to fend for yourself."

I didn't want to be stuck on the TransCanada Highway with no money and nowhere to go.

They gave me $50 in my pocket and put me on the train back to Toronto.

Chapter 25

HOMELESS

The first thing I did when I got back to the city was call the person who had the guy's $200. He still had it and I went to get it.

It was ten o'clock at night and I had fifty dollars Canadian in my pocket and another $200 American. All I wanted was to get high.

I ended up paying sixty dollars for a hotel room for the night. I kept enough for a second night at the hotel and I spent the rest on crack. There I was, just back from rehab, sitting in a hotel room and smoking crack.

The next day I called Brittany and told her that I had finished the program, was back in the city, and staying in a hotel. Because we had spent some time together on the day I was in Toronto, I figured maybe we could work it out. I mentioned that we'd been together for so long and had been so close. It turned out she just wanted be friends. She said she was dating another guy and we could hang out as friends.

My heart was so involved. I couldn't just "be friends" with

somebody that I had loved, slept with, and was going to marry. That wasn't going to work for me. Once it was over, it was over. Once she had been with somebody else, it kind of destroyed the intimacy and I felt I could never go back.

After two nights in the hotel, all of my money was gone. I was back on crack and I had no place to go.

That was the beginning of my days living on the street - sleeping in a hostel, panhandling, sleeping in the snow, being cold, lonely and basically just surviving by doing pills and heroin, and destroying myself once again.

I ended up in downtown Toronto, walking down Yonge Street. Somebody had mentioned a hostel down by Richmond and Yonge, so I thought, "Okay, maybe I'll walk down there, since I have nowhere else to go."

Fear crept over me because I didn't have a clue what was going to happen next, who I was going to run into, or how I was going to deal with the next situation.

I remember standing inside the telephone booth across the street from the hostel. I pushed my stem and I did the last little bit of resin that was left of my crack. Then I crossed the road to the shelter. I ended up getting in, spent the night, went out the next day and started panhandling.

That hostel had a drop-in centre. The next day, I went into the drop-in centre and slowly looked around to check out who was there. The people in the drop-in were from the area.

That experience was like a combination of my first day of school and my first day of incarceration. You scoped out the scene. You minded your own business and you didn't really jump in or become too sociable or aggressive. You sat back and went with the flow. You could tell who you might talk to and who you might not talk to.

Eventually you found acceptance and a new social circle started. As I said before, this happens in any new social situation.

At the drop-in I ran into someone who I knew from the east end. He was both shocked and happy to see me. We always got along and I was always an accepted person. Everybody has enemies, but for the most part, people liked me and knew I was a nice guy. So we hung out for a little bit and then went out panhandling.

It just so happened that there were people selling crack in the drop-in during the day. That's how my contacts with the local drug dealers began.

You've got to be careful down there because there are undercover cops that look worse than homeless people. I found this out periodically when someone was "taken down" or "jacked up." You get jacked up by someone who looks like they've been on the street for thirty years and they haven't taken a shower in a month. Then they show you their badge, their handcuffs and their gun.

It made me realize that I couldn't really trust anybody. That's why I always say that if I do something, I do it alone. That way the only person who can get caught is me, and the only person who can get me in trouble is me.

So I got into the drug scene heavy down there. My routine was to wake up at the hostel, eat breakfast, go out and panhandle. By the time the drop-in opened, I'd have twenty dollars - enough for twenty pieces of crack.

Then I would go back and forth all day - going out, panhandling, coming back, buying more crack. I did that all day and all night, until curfew came at the shelter. Then I'd do the whole thing all over again the next day.

113

As time went on, I began to meet and hang around with other people. Even after all this shit that I had been through up until that point, crack was still fun for me - even though it was killing me. Crack was just destroying my life. I didn't see it. I didn't want to see it. I didn't want to acknowledge anything like that.

Looking back, I realize how much money I was making and spending on drugs every day. Drugs were occupying my time and keeping me from being so bored.

Then I started missing the hostel curfew. The next thing you know, if you miss curfew at a hostel, you can't come in that night. You've got to try and be there by a certain time.

If you miss that time, there's a chance your bed is going to be taken. If your bed is taken, you have to come back again at midnight to see if there's another bed available. And then the cycle starts over again.

There were times when I came back after midnight and the hostel was full and I couldn't get in. Then what did I do? Well, I went back to panhandling. I found areas where there were people sleeping on the street at night.

Yonge Street at Dundas Street or Gerrard Street basically became my *panning ground* - my survival area where I would go to make my money.

I had contact with drug dealers from Yonge and King basically over to Sherbourne and up to Gerrard.

I immersed myself in the drug culture on the street. I never became close friends with people because, truly, deep down inside, I knew that I didn't want to make that my life. I didn't want to be on the street forever. I didn't want to be seventy, like you see some people on the street.

I always had that little bit of hope in the back of my head

that things might change and an opportunity might arise and my life would be better. I just didn't know when that would come, or if it would come. But I didn't want to totally shut the door on that.

Eventually, I began sleeping on the street and not in a hostel anymore. There would be certain people that I would crash with. It was always safer to sleep in numbers than alone, because you never knew what was going to happen at night.

There were crazy people out there and I knew of people who had been killed in their sleeping bags just because they were homeless.

Daniel's bed in a church doorway.

The view from Daniel's bed.

Chapter 26

LIFE ON THE STREET

As the days went on, I continued to panhandle. Maybe you even passed me on the street back then. I used to pan at Yonge and Elm Street. Once in a while, later at night, I panned at Yonge and Gerrard. On cold days, I panned inside the subway station, but the police usually kicked me out and ticketed me.

During the day, I often panned at Dundas and Victoria, in front of a donut shop. The donut shop was a very good spot right next to Ryerson University.

Sometimes students actually took the time to ask me questions. Some of them might have been doing projects for school, but once they started talking to me and realized that I had a bit of intellect, they tried to understand a little bit more.

Some people would help me out every single day. Sometimes, when other people were panning in my spot, they wouldn't give to them. The regulars told me they liked to stick with certain panhandlers, which I truly, truly appreciated.

I did take advantage of people, in the sense that I used some of the money for drugs, but I also used some of it for food. I never really asked for money. Instead, I always said, "Good morning, have a good day."

Some people would give me money and most wouldn't. As I said, I was never one of those guys who would sit in the same spot for eight hours straight. I would make enough money for whatever I needed. Then I would leave for an hour or so and then I would come back. I think a lot of people appreciated the fact that I wasn't there constantly - meaning eight hours with a lunch break, like working.

Not asking for money didn't make it any better, but I was always honest with people. For example, one day a lady handed me a $50 bill.

I said, "Thank you very, very much."

I stood up right away, because with fifty dollars I didn't need to be there anymore. Some people would still stay there, but they're just greedy and just want as much as they can get. So I started walking down the street and was picking up discarded cigarette butts.

The lady ran after me and then tapped me on the shoulder and she said, "Excuse me."

I said, "Yes?"

She said, "I just gave you fifty dollars. Why don't you go buy yourself a pack of cigarettes with the money instead of picking the dirty butts up off the street?"

I tried to explain to her that the money she had given me wasn't meant for cigarettes. It was meant for food or other stuff to help me survive. I told her that cigarettes were a luxury and I rarely bought cigarettes.

Now you're probably saying to yourself, "Oh yeah, you won't buy cigarettes, but you're buying crack or pills."

But I was buying drugs in order to survive. On the street

you get into a routine that helps you get by, especially when you're alone in the world.

Imagine that you don't have anybody to talk to, nobody cares about you, you don't know where anybody in your life is, you have no friends, and you don't have a roof over your head. You would have to do certain things every day just to survive.

It's the same thing with my addiction. At first it was fun. It was like being on a vacation. But then I had to go back to reality and survive. I mean, with nowhere to go - being outside, with no shelter, and no possessions - drugs were the things that helped me make it through the hours of the day. No matter how sick and demented that sounds, that was my learned behaviour.

Without my drugs, I probably would have lost my sanity. I'm sure I could have found other things to do, but remember, I already had this addiction prior to being on the street.

Another thing you have to realize is that all the programs you hear about for people like me aren't as readily available as you think.

Many people said, "So just go get a job."

If you think about it realistically - and this isn't an excuse or a cop-out - I was on the street with no fixed address, no driver's license, no nothing, I couldn't change my clothes or shower every day. Sometimes, I could only shower once a week, or once every two or three weeks.

You've got to look at it from the employer's side. What sort of employer wouldn't mind if their employee came to work every day in the same dirty clothes, or only took a shower every two or three weeks?

Also, most employers don't pay you until you've worked for two weeks or a month. How would you live until you got your first pay?

One summer while I was on the street, I tried working in construction and it was pretty hard.

Think about it this way: the night before work you have to pan enough to eat that night, and enough to eat the next day at work. You have to pan enough money to travel to work and get back from work. When you get back from work, you have to pan enough to eat, and then you have to do the same thing over and over and over again until you get paid.

What about getting to work in the middle of a snowstorm. There's nobody out there to help you when you're living on the street.

It's not like I made a lot of money panhandling. Sometimes I'd make $5.00, $6.00, or if I was lucky, $7.00 in an hour. Sometimes it was more and sometimes it was less.

What employer is going to say, "You know what - it's okay that Dan took the last three days off work because he's on the street. It was really cold and snowing or raining and nobody was out on the street to help him. Shouldn't we give him as much time off as he needs?"

My mom always encouraged me to work and couldn't understand why I resisted. She said that really, my life on the street was the same as a full-time job - getting up, panning for money, buying drugs, finding a place to sleep and then starting all over again the next day.

Panning

I pan the area
    Hat in hand
    Looking for a handout
    You offer me a hand up
    All I want is coin for smokes
    But you want my salvation
    Hands off
    Just leave me be
    Don't put your expectations onto me
    What's it to you
    If I'm a panhandler?
    .. by Dan's mom

Chapter 27

PANHANDLER REFLECTIONS

Panhandling was sometimes dangerous at night. Some kids who were out for a good time got drunk and rowdy and made fun of the homeless. Some homeless people tried to defend themselves verbally.

Those kids thought it was funny. The next thing you knew, those kids were following the homeless people to where they were asleep in their sleeping bags and stomping on them and beating the shit out of them, with not even a chance for them to get out and defend themselves.

It's sad. It's sick. And these people thought they were better than everybody else. They came from good families and rich homes. They end up being lawyers or doctors, or they end up taking care of your kids.

During the day, they work for humanity and all that sort of bullshit, but in true life, after they've had a few drinks in them, they don't give a shit about anything. They are just evil people who think they are better than everybody else. That was something that I didn't want to become from day one.

There it goes - back to beginning of my story, where I said I never wanted everything handed to me. I didn't want to be that sort of rich snob that you see on TV. I wanted to be from that down-to-earth, tight-knit TV family.

There were some kids in their first year of university who would walk by and say, "Get a job."

They didn't truly comprehend the fact that there were specific reasons why people were out there panhandling. There are very few people who actually choose to be on the street.

I mean, there were kids who were weekend warriors - the kids who ran away from home for the weekends and finally their parents just had enough and slammed the door on them and they were stuck out on the street.

In a sense that was by choice. But you know most of those kids eventually got back into their houses and they straightened out their lives. They realized that once the weekend was done, everyone else had gone home and they were stuck out there and didn't know how to survive on the street. They didn't have that sort of survival instinct. You don't have to be a smart person to know how to survive.

When I think about it, I have actually experienced and lived life at both ends of the spectrum.

When people made insulting comments to me, I used to have my little rebuttals and I think it used to shock them. You try to embarrass me and I'll try to do the same thing - tit for tat.

It surprised a lot of people that a street person like me had insight and ability. Some university kids who had never been away from home and were in residence thought they ran the world. They felt that they were better than everyone because they were educated and could get a good job.

They would say, "Go get a fucking job."

I'd say, "Listen, when your mom stops packing your cookies, takes away your emergency credit card, stops making your bed and doing your laundry for you, then come talk to me."

Then there were the little gangster-type guys who came hanging around acting all tough and laughing at us, with their girlfriends hanging on their arms, and all blinged-up in their fake jewellery. They thought they were better than you. They tried to make fun of you to look cool in front of their girlfriends.

I had rebuttals for them like, "Obviously, your life isn't that great either if you have nothing better to do than insult a homeless person."

Usually it got their friends to laugh at them and they kind of got embarrassed.

I had different rebuttals, but for the most part I took it. Same thing when you have to do certain grunt work at your job. You have to do what you have to do sometimes to survive, and I wasn't a violent person. I could be if I needed to be, but that wasn't something I tried to show people. Why? Because you don't want people to know all that sort of stuff. I tried to get by with who I was, not for what I could do to them.

Anyways, I don't judge people for what they're doing. I mean some people drink on the street because that's how they survive. I can't condemn anybody for what they do to survive.

Think about it for a minute. If the world came to an end, meaning the electricity was gone, or there was a war, who would be the ones surviving?

The people on the street know how to survive, how to find shelter, how to stay warm, how to find food, how to keep in shape. They know the places to sleep. That's why everybody can learn from everybody and if everybody helped everybody, then the world would be a lot better place.

These are the things you learn to live with on the street. It's not only the mental abuse, ignorant comments, or occasional physical abuse you get. You also have to deal with the violence and the fear of the police.

Chapter 28

PANHANDLING TICKETS

I remember one time when a police officer said he would arrest me for trespassing, but if I became a snitch, he wouldn't arrest me.

I said, "You're crazy; I wouldn't ever do anything like that."

He said, "Think about it. You are just a piece of puke to everybody else. Nobody cares about you. Why don't you start caring about yourself and helping us and that will help you? I'm sure you don't want to spend time in jail until your court date. No one else is going to get you out. Nobody cares about you. Look at you. You're a loser; you're homeless; you're a bum and you're on your own. Why not be smart?"

To me that sort of verbal abuse was kind of humorous. As long as you're strong inside and you believe in yourself, there's hope and nobody can tell you who and what you are. You can only make that so yourself.

Anyways, I turned him down and did my time in jail.

There were good police officers too. There was one officer who had a warrant to arrest me for "Failure to Appear." He knew I panhandled on Yonge Street. Before he arrested me, he dropped $5.00 in my hat and said, "Here's some money for the canteen when you're in jail. You can use it to buy some cigarettes."

I really appreciated that.

I was always polite when I panhandled. I didn't bother anybody or cause problems, but lots of times I got tickets from the police for *aggressive panhandling or encumbering the sidewalk.*

Where was I supposed to keep those tickets? How was I supposed to pay those fines? So I just shoved them in my pockets and ignored them. Sometimes I just threw them away.

There were dozens of tickets. The fines built up and there were lots of court dates that I missed because I was living on the street. I didn't have a phone, or a watch, or a calendar to write down the court dates. I just ignored them, hoping they would go away.

Eventually arrest warrants were issued by a judge for "Failure to Appear." That means they were issued because I didn't show up in court for my panhandling tickets. Sometimes months or years would pass before a warrant was issued for one ticket. Then I would get picked up and put in jail for a week, or two, or three. At least in jail, I had a roof over my head and food to eat.

How many times in one year can you get arrested for trivial stuff like that?

My time in jail didn't cancel the ticket fines from the City of Toronto. The amounts I owed continued to grow. With all those fines against my name, I could never get a driver's license, even if I got off the street.

Each time I got out of jail, I would go back to living on the street and panhandling. Finally, there were so many outstanding warrants for missing a bunch of court dates for panhandling tickets, that the police arrested me for a bunch of outstanding warrants at once. My lawyer stepped in and had all the arrest warrants for "Failure to Appear" put together into one sentence.

In the fall of 2006, I ended up doing 90 days in Penetang Jail. While I was there, I went on the Methadone Program to control my opiates urges.

My parents visited me a few times and they saw a change in my attitude and heard a change in my voice. I really did want to change. I guess when you're sitting in jail and sober on methadone, you want to take over the world. I felt that I could do anything and that everything was going to be different.

I didn't want to go back to living on the street and I know my parents couldn't stand the stress of having me homeless and living on the street again.

Chapter 29

CHANCE TO START OVER

When I got out of jail I had a chance to start my life all over again in a small city that was an hour and a half from downtown Toronto. My parents found me a place in Barrie in a townhouse complex where lots of young families lived.

My parents became my landlords. My sister and parents and some of their friends donated second-hand furniture for my place. I was still taking daily methadone to control my cravings. I got social assistance to start over again. I signed a lease to pay my parents $400 a month rent from my cheque and I and also signed a letter agreeing to rules about my behaviour.

I knew only one person who lived in Barrie. I met him when I was in jail in Penetang. He wasn't a hard core drug user, but he did use. We started hanging out together. It only took me a few weeks before I was right back to shooting rockets - a 200 mg. morphine pill - and trying to find crack. Before I knew it a whole bunch of people were hanging out at my place doing drugs.

Soon I was lying to my parents and hiding my drugs when they came to visit. I could only fool them for a short time.

One day, my parents came up to visit and my dad offered to take me food shopping to No Frills. My mom stayed at my place and waited for us.

When my dad and I came back, my mom didn't say anything and they left. After they were gone, I went to get the chess box where I had hidden my drugs. I was going to get some crack, but the box was completely empty. All my syringes, my crack pipe and my crack were gone.

Obviously, while we were gone, my mom - being a very caring person - snooped around to make sure I was doing okay. She must have found my drug stash in my chess box and emptied it and took it away to have it checked, instead of confronting me right then and having a huge fight.

My parents figured out what was going on. Despite my denials, they had the proof. By that time, there were people living all over my place, on my couch and in my basement. People were coming in and out all the time, eating my food, using drugs, and making a mess of the place. I just took a small community of townhouses in a nice family area and basically brought in the downtown Toronto drug mentality. This destroyed the peace and quiet in that little community while I was there.

My parents took me to an addiction doctor in Barrie and he suggested that they cut ties with me and let me sink to the bottom. And that's what my parents finally did.

My father and mother said, "Enough is enough."

Soon after, my parent's sent me a legal eviction letter. They gave me notice that I had to move out on a certain date. Then, when I didn't leave by that date, they sent a security company to get everybody, including me, out of the place.

There I was, less than four months later, evicted with no money, no place to live, and no place to go. Everybody who was supposed to be my friend was gone. Nobody gave a shit about me when I wasn't supplying them with a place to do their drugs.

My mother came to see me one last time. She took me to the local bus station, bought me a one-way bus ticket back to Toronto. She gave me a sleeping bag and a knapsack and $80 for one night in a cheap room.

She knew I would end up back on the street and I could see that it was killing her. Just before I got on the bus, she hugged me and she told me to take care of myself and that she and my dad hoped that I would choose to get help for my addictions and decide to change.

That hurt for a bit, but by the time the bus was halfway back to Toronto, I started thinking about that $80 that was burning a hole in my pocket.

When I got back to the city, instead of going straight to sign into a detox centre, I bought drugs at the bus station. Then I walked the two blocks to my old panhandling spot at Yonge and Elm by Pizza Pizza.

I went around and said "Hi" to the store owners and to the people I knew on the street. Then I started the old panhandling cycle all over again.

In May 2006, I returned to living on the streets in Toronto. My daily routine consisted of panhandling, eating occasionally, picking up cigarette butts, smoking, doing drugs, pills, cocaine powder, and smoking crack.

I was sleeping here, there and everywhere. At one point, I

found a box in an alley off Yonge Street. The box was up high and out of the way.

I didn't really let anybody know that I was there because when you're on the street it's very dangerous to tell anybody where you're sleeping. Anything can happen to you in your sleep. You never know who is jealous of you on the street. You never know who is out to get you, or who doesn't like you. It's stupid, childhood playground stuff in an environment of hopelessness, dangerous drugs, crime and violence.

That's basically what it was like. The most childish thing could upset somebody you didn't even know. So you never let anybody know where you were sleeping.

The owners of the place knew I was there and they tried to get rid of me, not in a physical or violent way. They let me understand that the box was above a stairway and if the box gave out, something bad might have happened to me. They said they would be liable, and they wouldn't want to come to work and find out that I was dead.

I didn't really want that either, but I kept going back and they kept kicking me out, until finally they nailed the box shut.

From there I moved to another place on the steps of an old church on Shuter Street by Church Street. I slept there for a while.

Other times, I just didn't sleep. I'd be lucky if I got eight hours every week. I would go for days and days doing coke, and stuff like that, and I wouldn't sleep until my body shut down. Literally, I'd be sitting down and I'd shut my eyes for a second and I'd wake up two hours later. That's total exhaustion.

No matter how little sleep I got, I was out trying to make money in order to get some more dope. That's the abuse and the damage that I gave to my body.

Chapter 30

STREETS TO HOME

Winter was coming in a couple of months. I could feel the air changing. I was sick of my life and dreaded another winter outside.

Suddenly, I realized how truly alone I was on the street. I was afraid of spending the rest of my life alone, with nobody to keep me company, or check on me to make sure I was okay. No matter how long it had been since I had seen my parents, I always knew that I could just call and hear their voices. That was a comfort and part of what kept me going. My parents were my little glimpse of heaven when there was nobody else out there who cared about me. I decided to call my parents just to hear their voices. My parents were getting older. I asked my mom what would happen to me if they were gone and I died on the street. Where would I be buried? Who would make sure I had a funeral? I started to think about stuff like that.

When you're on the street, it takes time to get help. You have to be ready. You have to pace yourself. You can't expect to jump to the finish line and expect everything to be hunky-dory. You have to take little baby steps and do things right. That way you have a solid foundation to move forward. There were decent places to go to for help, like The Works and Streets to Home. They had people who listened and tried to help people like me work things through.

The staff members at The Works were just great. They had needle exchanges, crack kits, and harm-reduction programs. They helped prevent the spread of diseases. They helped addicts like me get onto the Methadone Program, if that's what they wanted. They understood that if people were going to continue to do drugs, then they might as well be safe. At The Works, you decided what you needed. The counsellors at The Works gave me hope. There should be more places like that so the schoolyards are clean, so people aren't leaving dirty needles around, so addicts and homeless people are being responsible enough to get on welfare and get money to live indoors and the help they need to take care of themselves.

At the time when I decided to leave the street, there was a new agency called Streets to Homes. An outreach worker came by a few times to talk to me where I was sleeping in the doorway of the old church at Shuter and Church. She told me that their job was to help homeless people find permanent housing. She asked if I needed help to find a safe place to live. Still being stubborn, at first I said, "No." After a while, I decided to go their office, which was nearby. I decided I was finally ready for some help to get off the street. Without the help of the workers at Streets to Home and The Works, some people, including me, wouldn't have had the opportunity to receive a helping hand to try and start over.

At thirty-three years of age, I was finally ready to make a change in my life. Obviously, I would make mistakes and unpleasant things would happen, but think about what I went through for all those years. Making the odd mistake and trying to fix it was worth it. Now that I look back on my life, I say,

"Holy shit, I was pretty crazy! I have nothing to show for all those lost years."

As I remember all of this, it's really hard. It makes me think a lot and worry about what lies ahead. It also makes me want to use again and forget. I'm like a new baby, so to speak, hopefully reborn into a different lifestyle. I have to make grownup decisions. I don't have the luxury of making the childhood mistakes that I made before. Now the mistakes that I make could cost me my life and my relationships with my family. I don't know how I'm going to manage, or how well I'm going to do, but I'm going to try my best.

So finally, I went through Streets to Homes to get their help. I didn't care how big or small my place was. I just wanted to be safe and off the street. I called my parents to tell them what I was doing.

I could hear the surprise and relief in their voices.

The outreach worker at Streets to Home helped me find a small room in an apartment in the basement of a low-rise apartment building in the west end of the city, near the Lakeshore, between Kipling and Brown's Line. It was a far trek from my previous area at Yonge and Dundas. It took me right out of my element.

The outreach worker helped me get on welfare and get direct payment of the rent to my landlord, so I couldn't spend my rent money and get evicted again.

Thanks to the doctor and counsellors at The Works, I got on methadone and went to the pharmacy every day to get my drink. It helped me feel better. I didn't have urges or bad dreams, and I stopped getting sick.

Once every week or two, I took the streetcar and subway downtown to my doctor at The Works. In order to get downtown, it was a good hour, or longer, each way. Sometimes that journey in itself was hard, because when I got down there, I was tempted to be up to my old tricks.

The counsellors at The Works welcomed me and encouraged me. They knew that I would make slips and I did.

After a few months, my parents saw big changes in me and they decided to help me get an apartment very close to their place. My mom and dad became more than a mom and dad. They became my best friends.

One day, my mom took me to the Humane Society to pick a pet, so I wouldn't ever be alone. I picked a tiny abandoned kitten. He looked me in the eye and licked my fingers and I felt an instant connection in my heart. I called him T.J. He is like my baby boy. He's still with me and I make sure he has everything he needs.

My life changed 100% for the better.

I truly want to straighten out my life and have a good relationship with my parents and sister. I just want to tell my story for me, and for my parents and sister who always stood by me and loved me.

I'm learning that I matter and I believe that the things I went through, I went through for a reason.

I know there was a purpose to my life and hopefully that purpose is to help other people who are in the same situation by telling my story. Then I will know that my life wasn't in vain.

Then I will know that my life is worth more than absolutely nothing.

Daniel

Daniel
with his
sister

Daniel and Evelyn Pollock, 2014

AFTERWORD

In the fall of 2007, soon after my son Daniel came off the streets of Toronto, I gave him a tape recorder and cassette tapes and encouraged him to dictate his story. It was my hope that by sharing his story of addiction and homelessness, Daniel would reflect on his life and realize that, despite his difficult journey, his life had meaning.

At first he resisted, but after several weeks he called to say his story was finished and he wanted me to listen to the tapes. This book is drawn from those tapes. It tells the story of his life, from his perspective, from birth until the age of 33.

In 2014, we released the first edition of the book and presented it to Daniel for his 40th birthday. Although his struggles continued, he was happy, and lived in a stable environment with his cat, T.J. for many years.

My hope was that this book would be part of his healing journey and would also help other families who faced similar challenges.

Evelyn N. Pollock, Daniel's Mother

Eternal Flame
Sculpture by Daniel S. Pollock
April 24, 1974 - September 15, 2017

FINAL FAREWELL

Daniel died unexpectedly of an accidental drug overdose on Friday, September 15, 2017, at the age of 43.

There will be no more fear of that dreaded phone call and no more secrets. We thank everyone who played a positive role in his life.

From early childhood Daniel had a zest for adventure. He was impulsive, fun-loving, and fiercely independent. Although Daniel's life was not easy, the one thing he always knew for sure, every day of his life, was that he was truly and deeply loved by us and by his sister, and that we were always there for him, no matter what.

David and I are so very grateful that Daniel was our son and that we were chosen for this roller-coaster journey as his parents. Because we loved him so deeply and we loved one another so much, we were able to endure the ups and downs together, and to tell his story - to make sure he is remembered as a kind, carefree human being, who was absolutely loving and loyal to his family and friends.

Dan & Karen

Dearest Daniel:

It was on the fifth day your life that we held you in our arms for the first time. Your dad and I fell in love with you immediately. I was 26 and Dad was 28 when we became your parents. It was our dream and our destiny.

You would be ours forever - so tiny, so beautiful, so perfect, with a full head of platinum blond hair and sparkling blue eyes. You cuddled into us and we knew immediately, that no matter what, we would protect you and love you forever and ever and always.

The doctor told us you were in the 90% percentile for height - that you would be tall when you grew up. And that was true. Somehow, when we weren't looking, you sprouted to 6'3". Your height came too early for your age and convinced you that you were an adult before you were ready.

Your grandparents adored you. It was reciprocal and un-conditional love - the kind of love every child deserves, and you and your sister experienced. Your little sister looked up to you and followed you around like a puppy. You became her protector, watched out for her, and filled this role all of your life. Later, your sister became your protector, your confidante, your best friend. You trusted and loved her more than anyone could imagine.

This past year (2017) you were so happy with yourself. You were settled in your own mobile home in a park in downtown Orillia. T.J. was your room mate. He was the cat you adopted ten years ago at the Toronto Humane Society when you first came off the street. That's when you dictated your story for me.

T.J. is safe with us now.

This year you bonded with the retired couple next door. Every morning you opened your kitchen curtains to signal to them that you were awake. Then you brewed your morning coffee and joined them on their porch for a coffee and a smoke. Throughout the week, your neighbour brought you apple crumble, muffins, or fruit salad. You chatted with another neighbour across the road. Other neighbours waved to you as they passed by; you waved back and asked how they were. For the first time in your adult life, dear Daniel, you felt accepted and part of a community. Until Friday morning, September 15th.

For many years we had dreaded the telephone call that came that Friday morning. It was so unexpected, since your life was going so well.

We will never forget the tenderness of our last week together:

Remember last Sunday? You rode your bike to the marina to surprise Dad and wash our boat, before he arrived. As Dad pulled up, you laughed and quipped, "Hey, Dad! I'm just protecting my inheritance!" You two spent the rest of the afternoon cruising Lake Couchiching, laughing and nibbling on sandwiches.

On Tuesday, Dad stopped by your house to say good-bye. He was leaving the next morning for a trip to Vancouver. As you hugged, you said, "I love you, Pops." Little did Dad know it would be your last hug.

On Wednesday morning you surprised me outside my writers' group meeting in town. We hugged, then with a big grin on your face you rode off on your bike, singing: "I love you, love you, love you Mom." You had just left your meeting with your Canadian Mental Health Association addiction counsellor. You had religiously attended counselling appointments for three years, and it seemed to be working.

Later, I picked you up and we went for lunch. In the restaurant you leaned over with a twinkle in your eye and asked:

"Tell me Mom, how do you really feel about our trip to Alberta to visit my birth mother next week? She's not my real mother you know. You are, and Dad's my real father. I just want to meet her and my half-brother to get some closure."

We already had airplane tickets. You were excited. You were going to meet them face-to-face, after being in telephone contact with them for several years.

You leaned in again and sang: "You know I love you, love you, love you Mom."

On Thursday morning, I dropped you at your very *last* probation appointment *ever* (you promised). Later that afternoon, you were working in your front garden, enjoying the sunshine and smiling. I know this, because you phoned me three times to describe the invasive Hosta roots you were pulling out. You said you were going to replace them with a colourful perennial next spring.

At 6:30 P.M., you were still in your garden. You called to tell me you had taken three of your limestone sculptures and arranged them in the soil around the space left by the Hosta.

You see, at age 41, you discovered your hidden talent for stone sculpting. Though I had to drag you with me to the sculpture studio the first time, you were immediately enthralled by the effect power tools had on stone. We continued to spend one day a week sculpting together in the warm weather. You had an incredible ability to create unique, geometric stone sculptures. The instructor became your mentor and friend.

Daniel poses with his sculpture, "Solitude", at the launch of Artful Canada artistique, a bilingual, heritage art book commemorating Canada's 150th birthday. Two of his sculptures are featured in the book.

The next morning, Friday, you were supposed to finish building your new front deck with the help of your neighbours. When you didn't slide open your curtains and come outside for your morning coffee, they used the extra key you had entrusted to them to open the door.

And that's when the dreaded phone call came.

We know there is nothing we could have done differently to avoid this sudden end. If we had a choice to go back and change the fact that you were our son, we would both make the same decision we made on that beautiful day 43 years ago - to embrace you, nurture and love you, stand behind you, and carry you in our hearts forever and ever. We were the parents you were meant to have and you were the son we were meant to have. We know you loved us with all your heart and that you never, ever, blamed us for any choices you made.

Dearest Daniel,

We will always love you. We will love you forever and always. We will miss your smile, your laughter, your company, your frequent phone calls, your sense of adventure and your love.

We LOVE YOU, LOVE YOU, LOVE YOU.

Mom, Dad, and Karen

Daniel with his father, sister and mother.

**Daniel poses beside his sculpture,
"Phenomenon",**

**Daniel's final sculpture,
"The Eternal Flame"
August, 2017**

150